The Complete Time Waster

FIREFLY BOOKS

A FIREFLY BOOK

Published by Firefly Books Ltd. 2009

First printing

Publisher Cataloging-in-Publication Data (U.S.)

Saunders, Eric.
The complete time waster / Eric Saunders.
[400] p. : col. ill. ; cm.
Summary: Puzzles, including crosswords, word games, trivia and facts, to amuse, perplex and entertain.
ISBN-13: 978-1-55407-454-9 (pbk.)
ISBN-10: 1-55407-454-1 (pbk.)
1. Puzzles. 2. Games. 3. Crossword puzzles. 1. Title.
793.73 dc22   GV1493.S276 2009

Library and Archives Canada Cataloguing in Publication

Saunders, Eric
The complete time waster / Eric Saunders.

ISBN-13: 978-1-55407-454-9
ISBN-10: 1-55407-454-1

1. Puzzles. 1. Title.

GV1493.S37815 2009   793.73   C2008-906377-5

Published in the United States by
Firefly Books (U.S.) Inc.
P.O. Box 1338, Ellicott Station
Buffalo, New York 14205

Published in Canada by
Firefly Books Ltd.
66 Leek Crescent
Richmond Hill, Ontario L4B 1H1

Printed in China

The publisher gratefully acknowledges the financial support for our publishing program by the Government of Canada through the Book Publishing Industry Development Program.

Puzzle compilation, typesetting and design by:

Puzzle Press Ltd
http://www.puzzlepress.co.uk

with additional material by Diane Law

TOTAL CONCENTRATION

Can you fill in the missing numbers so that each row, each column and two longest diagonal lines meet the totals given?

							69
1	5	15	9	6	14	11	61
4	20	10	16	15	18	3	86
13	9	6	20	11	12	14	83
1	19	9	4	18	9	9	79
7	10	17	13	6	10	16	79
14	6	20	5	17	13	8	83
2	8	3	12	19	5	3	52
42	75	80	79	92	91	64	53

WORD LADDER

Change one letter at a time (but not the position of any letter) to make a new word – and move from the word at the top of the ladder to the word at the bottom using the exact number of rungs provided.

L O S T
L I S T
M I S T
M I N T
M I N E
M I M E
T I M E

STARTING LINE

Which three-letter word can be placed at the start, to form three seven-letter words?

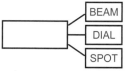

- BEAM
- DIAL
- SPOT

WEATHER for OPTIMISTS

Today the weather will be:

Wonderfully heartwarming, despite the hailstorms.

PICK 'N' MIX

Choose three words to describe your garden:

Green	Landscaped
Bonkers	Noisy
Scruffy	Chaotic
Clean	Minimal
Peaceful	Bland

TIED UP AT PRESENT

Which boy is holding the string attached to the present?

A B C

TWO DOWN

Fit five of the seven listed words into the Across rows in the grid, so that the other two words read down the shaded columns numbered 2 and 3.

ANKLE	ELATE
HEART	LEMON
SMEAR	TOPIC
	TRAIL

IN CHAINS

This chain of letters contains the names of three countries. The letters are in the correct order but need to be picked out.

YUERTUMGOUEAGYNO

_____   _____

_____

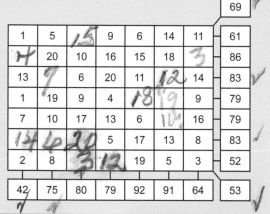

1

CLOCKWORDS

It's a race against the clock… How many common words of three or more different letters can you make from those on the clock face (without using plurals, proper nouns or abbreviations) in ten minutes? All words must contain BOTH the letters indicated by the hands on the clock.

QUOTE OF THE DAY

"Blessed is he who expects nothing, for he shall never be disappointed."
Benjamin Franklin

WEATHER for PESSIMISTS

Today the weather will be:

Sunny: bright enough to hurt your eyes

DICEY ARITHMETIC

Using three of the arithmetical signs ÷, −, x and +, can you achieve the correct total?

    =

BERMUDA TRIANGLE

Travel through the 'Bermuda Triangle' by visiting one room at a time and collecting a letter from each. You can enter the outside passageway as often as you like, but can only visit each room once. When you've completed your tour, the 15 letters spell out a word.

PROVERBS AND SAYINGS

The letters on the tiles were once all in place, but dropped out, falling in a straight line into the lower grid. Some tiles dropped earlier than others, so those on the lowest row aren't all from the same row in the grid above. Can you put them back into position in order to reveal a well-known proverb or saying?

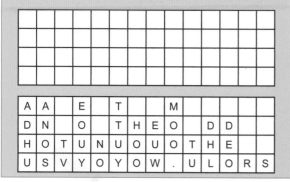

A	A		E		T			M		
D	N		O		T	H	E	O		D	D
H	O	T	U	N	U	O	U	O	T	H	E
U	S	V	Y	O	Y	O	W	.	U	L	O	R	S

JOIN THE DOTS

MISSING LINKS

Which word links the one on the left with the one on the right? We've done the first one, and when you've finished them all, the first letters of the link words will spell another word.

QUICK	**SAND**	CASTLE
HOME		WINE
MAKE		THROWN
BLOOD		JUICE
WARM		RUNNER

MUSIC TRIVIA

Who wrote the Sinead O'Connor hit *Nothing Compares 2 U*?

LETTER TRACKER

Begin in the central shaded square and follow a continuous path which will track from square to square, up, down and sideways, but never diagonally.

Your trail should cover every letter once only, in order to find:

Twenty drinks.

I	S	K	E	Y	O	A	L	V	O	S
H	K	D	O	V	C	C	A	A	D	P
W	A	O	N	G	O	N	I	C	R	O
D	O	R	A	E	C	I	F	O	T	G
R	N	R	M	A	R	T	F	E	N	I
E	P	E	G	A	L	O	C	E	D	A
H	Y	P	P	A	N	G	N	U.	Q	I
C	R	S	B	R	H	C	A	I	R	I
N	R	E	H	A	N	S	C	I	A	C
U	L	I	S	Y	D	O	M	L	T	O
P	K	M	E	D	A	N	E	L	K	C

SWEET BAD MUSIC

So who on earth was responsible for this lyric?

"If I was a sculptor
But then again, no"

MISSING LETTERS

One letter of the alphabet is missing from each box. Find them all and place them in the order of the numbered boxes to reveal a six-letter word.

Word: _____

1	2	3
JUOCI	PHYOE	TIYDP
NVSFB	QIGLC	GUOEQ
MTKYA	ZDUMV	JFZHR
XPZGD	FSWNK	MLXAS
WLQEH	RTXBJ	KVWNC

4	5	6
UDTKG	LVHWP	LVNEH
JSMHP	XJUCO	UWMFA
NWIQZ	TYDKG	BZGSI
REFLC	ESMQB	COJYR
VAXYO	RZANF	KPXDQ

Answers to puzzles on the previous page

Dicey Arithmetic: The signs are −, x and +.
Bermuda Triangle: ANTHROPOLOGISTS
Proverbs and Sayings: Do unto others as you would have them do unto you.

3

BOX CLEVER

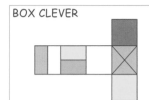

When the above is folded to form a cube, which one of the following can be produced?

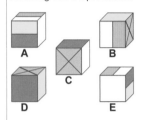

A   B   C   D   E

WORDWHEEL

Using only the letters in the Wordwheel, you have ten minutes to find as many words as possible, none of which may be plurals, foreign words or proper nouns. Each word must be of three letters or more, all must contain the central letter and letters can only be used once in every word. There is at least one nine-letter word in the wheel.

Nine-letter word: _____

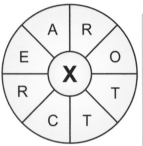

LAST MINUTE EXCUSES

In one minute, how many excuses can you find for:

Eating a whole cheesecake

TOP TEN

LAMB ☐
BEEF ☐
CHICKEN ☐
VEAL ☐
PORK ☐
PHEASANT ☐
VENISON ☐
GOAT ☐
RABBIT ☐
DUCK ☐

CHARACTER ASSIGNATION

Fill in the answers to the clues, across the grid. Then read down the diagonal line of seven squares, to reveal:
The title of a play by Shakespeare.

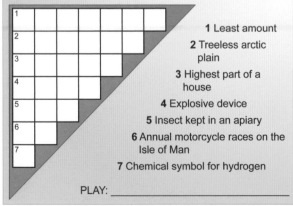

1 Least amount
2 Treeless arctic plain
3 Highest part of a house
4 Explosive device
5 Insect kept in an apiary
6 Annual motorcycle races on the Isle of Man
7 Chemical symbol for hydrogen

PLAY: _____

WHATEVER YOU DO, don't even THINK about...

Any of the following songs:

The Final Countdown
The Wizard of Oz
Delilah
Climb Ev'ry Mountain

SPELLING TEST

Which is the correctly spelled word?

QUESTIONNAIRE ☐
QUESTIONAIRE ☐
QUESTIONAIR ☐

Answers to puzzles on the previous page

Missing Links: Sand, Port, Over, Orange, Front. Thus: SPOOF
Music Trivia: Prince
Letter Tracker: Lager, Martini, Coffee, Cognac, Schnapps, Brandy, Sherry, Pernod, Whiskey, Vodka, Orange, Cocoa, Calvados, Port, Gin, Daiquiri, Cocktail, Lemonade, Milk, Punch.
Sweet Bad Music: Elton John *Your Song* (lyrics written by Bernie Taupin)
Missing Letters: RABBIT

BROKEN-HEARTED

Don't be halfhearted in your attempts to get these couples back together again! Match both sides of each heart, to reveal their names.

_____ & _____   _____ & _____   _____ & _____

_____ & _____   _____ & _____   _____ & _____

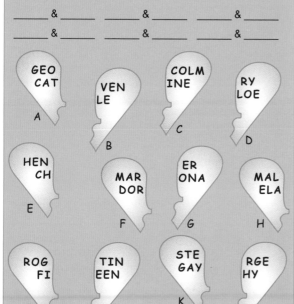

A — GEO CAT

B — VEN LE

C — COLM INE

D — RY LOE

E — HEN CH

F — MAR DOR

G — ER ONA

H — MAL ELA

I — ROG FI

J — TIN EEN

K — STE GAY

L — RGE HY

EGG TIMER

Can you complete this puzzle in the time it takes to boil an egg? The answers to the clues are anagrams of the words immediately above and below, plus or minus a letter.

1 Second working day
2 Remained
3 Bread raising agent
4 Chair
5 Showy garden flower
6 Looked at intently
7 Baked in an oven

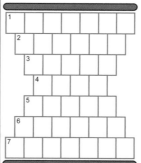

ODD ONE OUT

Which one is different to the rest?

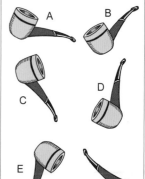

A   B   C   D   E   F

Answers to puzzles on the previous page

Box Clever: B
Wordwheel: The nine-letter word is EXTRACTOR
Character Assignation: 1 Minimum, 2 Tundra, 3 Attic, 4 Bomb, 5 Bee, 6 TT, 7 H.
Play: *Macbeth*.
Spelling Test: QUESTIONNAIRE

ON THE TILES

In this puzzle, the eight tiles on the right must be fitted into the pattern in the middle so as to form four words reading across and five words reading down. No tile may be rotated!

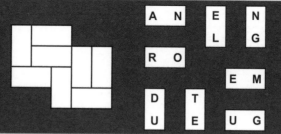

LOOSE VOWELS

Someone has taken all the vowels out of what was once a completed crossword. Can you put them all back in again? You should use only those letters beneath the grid.

S	K			S				L
C		G				R		
		L					R	
L				T	H			
	G					B		
			C		K			W
P		P		T			R	
			D			G		R
		T		M			T	S

A A A A A A A A

E E E E E E E E E E E E

I I I I I

O O O O O O O O O

A MATCHING PAIR

Which are the only two socks that are identical in every way?

TOP FIVE

Best places to live:

1 _____

2 _____

3 _____

4 _____

5 _____

Answers to puzzles on the previous page

Broken-hearted: A and L, E and D, F and J, H and C, I and G, K and B.
Egg Timer: 1 Tuesday, 2 Stayed, 3 Yeast, 4 Seat, 5 Aster, 6 Stared, 7 Roasted.
Odd One Out: B – It has a shorter stem.

DESIGN YOUR OWN

HERB GARDEN

PAIR SHAPES

In the box below there are shapes in three different colors, red, white and blue. Any shape may have been rotated, but can you see which is the only shape to appear exactly twice in exactly the same color?

REAL WORDS

Which is the real word?

Lollygotious ☐

Liripipe ☐

Lollynoxious ☐

STARTER LETTER

Write down one each of the listed items, all of which must begin with the starter letter:

E

Country	
Tree	
Boy's name	
Girl's name	
River	
City	
Animal	
Make of car	
Drink	

CROSSED WORDS

Using only the letters above the diagram, fill in the squares to make a common two-word phrase, one word reading down and the other across.

A C C D I K T

PRE-FAME NAME GAME

By what name do we know this famous person?

Barry Alan Pincus

WHAT DOES IT MEAN?

What is the meaning of the word

Erinaceous

Answer: _____

Answers to puzzles on the previous page

On the Tiles:

T	U	G		
E	R	O	D	E
A	N	N	U	L
		G	E	M

A Matching Pair: B and C

Loose Vowels:

S	K	I	E	S		A	I	L
C	O	G		O	A	R		E
A	I	L		O		E	R	E
L		O	A	T	H		O	
E	G	O				B	E	E
	O		C	A	K	E		W
P	O	P		T		I	R	E
I		A	D	O		G	A	R
E	A	T		M	E	E	T	S

7

CODEWORD

This is a crossword puzzle in code. Every number represents a different letter of the alphabet and this number remains the same throughout the puzzle. Use the letters either side of the grid as well as the check-box below the grid to keep a track on your progress.

A
B
C
D
E
F
G
H
I
J
K
L
M

5	23	9	12	16	1	22	■	24	8	12	12	10	2	4
10	■	12	■	17	■	20	17	13	■	■	20	■	20	■
11	7	16	6	16	■	18	■	13	7	13	21	16	22	13
13	■	18	■	9	13	3	20	22	■	■	13	■	1	■
4	11 P	16	12	13	■	13	■	■	11	12	13	13	1
■	13 E	■	18	16	12	22	20	1	20	■	■	4	■
25	12 R	20	18	23	■	■	1	■	22	12	13	4	4
■	26	■	8	■	4	13	12	20	24	■	11	■	13
14	8	20	17	19	13	1	■	8	■	16	7	10	8	9
■	12	■	8	■	■	20	22	4	■	7	■	15	■	16
25	23	18	4	7	20	11	■	5	16	7	17	23	10	1

N
O
P
Q
R
S
T
U
V
W
X
Y
Z

1	2	3	4	5	6	7	8	9	10	11	12	13
										P	R	E

14	15	16	17	18	19	20	21	22	23	24	25	26

A IS TO B

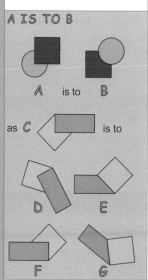

A   is to   B

as C   is to

D

E

F

G

ARRANGING THINGS

If you fit six of these seven words into the grid, the word left over will appear reading down the shaded squares.

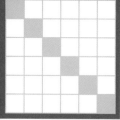

BAMBOO   BELFRY
BORROW   IODINE
SHRIMP   SEESAW
TAURUS

Answers to puzzles on the previous page

Pair Shapes: ✳
Real Words: ✳
Liripipe
Crossed Words: Card trick
Pre-fame Name Game: Barry Manilow
What Does It Mean?: Like a hedgehog

EYE-SPY

I spy with my little eye something beginning with:

_____

MIRROR WRITING

Write this word upside down:

TUESDAY

_____

DO YOU KNOW…

…what happened in New York on this date?

24 October 1931

PRE-FAME NAME GAME

By what name do we know this famous person?

Shirley Beaty

_____

COMPLETE THIS LIMERICK:

A young man who lives in our town

Once felt quite decidedly 'down'

He said "To cheer up

I must drink a cup…"

_____

SWEET BAD MUSIC

So who on earth was responsible for this lyric?

"Lucky that my breasts
Are small and humble
So you don't confuse
Them with mountains"

DOMINADDITION

Can you place the remaining dominoes in their correct positions, so that the total number of spots in each of the four rows and five columns equals the sum at the end of that row or column?

= 17
= 19
= 13
= 7

= 17 = 16 = 10 = 11 = 2

WHO AM I?

Shut it now, honey!

I am:

_____

Answers to puzzles on the previous page

A is to B: E – The top shape moves to the back, then the whole makes a 180 degrees turn.

Arranging Things:
Across (from the top): Belfry, Iodine, Shrimp, Taurus, Bamboo, Seesaw.
Down: Borrow.

Codeword:

H	Y	D	R	A	N	T		F	U	R	R	O	W	S
O		R		C		I	C	E		I		I		I
P	L	A	Z	A		M		E	L	E	V	A	T	E
E		M		D	E	B	I	T			E		N	
S	P	A	R	E		E			P	R	E	E	N	
		E		M	A	R	T	I	N	I		S		
G	R	I	M	Y			N		T	R	E	S	S	
	J		U		S	E	R	I	F		P		E	
Q	U	I	C	K	E	N		U		A	L	O	U	D
	R		U			I	T	S	L		X		A	
G	Y	M	S	L	I	P		H	A	L	C	Y	O	N

9

TWO-WORD HOROSCOPES

Aries – stop it

Taurus – dear me

Gemini – run... now!

Cancer – simply pointless

Leo – secret meeting

Virgo – not again!

Libra – you loser

Scorpio – lost cause

Sagittarius – daft outfit

Capricorn – forget it

Aquarius – don't bother

Pisces – can't happen

SHAPE RECOGNITION

Which are the only three pieces which will fit together to form a copy of this black shape?

A   B

C   D

E   F

G

H

I

SECRET MISSION

Your secret mission (should you choose to accept it) is:

To try to influence the world's stock markets by starting random internet stories.

REAL WORDS

Which is the real word?

Deitantious ☐

Ditteany ☐

Diaglyph ☐

ALL AT SEA

Which famous ship was damaged by fire in May 2007 while undergoing restoration at Greenwich in London?

HEXAGONY

Can you place the hexagons in the grid, so that where any triangle touches another along a straight line, the contents of both are the same? One triangle is already filled.

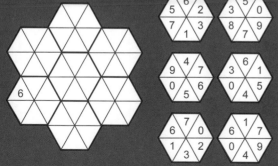

PRE-FAME NAME GAME

By what name do we know this famous person?

Leonard Slye

_____

MUSIC TRIVIA

Which pop singer did Debbie Rowe marry?

SNAKES AND LADDERS

This is a standard game, so when you land at the foot of a ladder, you climb it; and when you land on the head of a snake, you slide down its tail. You need to throw an exact number to land on 100 to win – counting backwards if you don't, eg if you land on 98 and throw a five, you will end up on 97. The dice is thrown for you and always lands in this recurring order: 5, 2, 3, 4, 1, 6, so you can start by immediately placing your counter on square 5. Good luck – hope you win!

100	99	98	97	96	95	94	93	92	91
81	82	83	84	85	86	87	88	89	90
80	79	78	77	76	75	74	73	72	71
61	62	63	64	65	66	67	68	69	70
60	59	58	57	56	55	54	53	52	51
41	42	43	44	45	46	47	48	49	50
40	39	38	37	36	35	34	33	32	31
21	22	23	24	25	26	27	28	29	30
20	19	18	17	16	15	14	13	12	11
1	2	3	4	5	6	7	8	9	10

TANGLED TACKLE

Which of these anglers has landed the fish?

A   B   C

PATCHWORK

Fit the letters A, B, C, D, E and F into the grid below, so that every horizontal row, every vertical column and every shape of six smaller squares contain six different letters. Some are already in place.

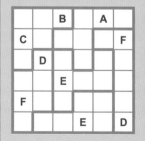

MOVIE QUOTES

We give you a line, you tell us who said it and the film:

"I'm not going to waste my time arguing with a man who's lining up to be a hot lunch. That's a twenty footer!"

WHERE ON *HEART* ?

Where on Earth is Blue Ball?

Answer: _____

QUOTE OF THE DAY

"Anyone who has never made a mistake has never tried anything new."
Albert Einstein

Answers to puzzles on the previous page

Shape Recognition:
A, D and F
Real Words: Diaglyph
All at Sea: *The Cutty Sark*
Pre-fame Name Game: Roy Rogers
Music Trivia: Michael Jackson

Hexagony:

		3	6	1		
	3	5	0	4	5	6	2
8	7	9	4	7	7	1	3
6	7	0	5	6	6	1	7
1	3	2	5	0	4	9
	8	1	4		

11

DICE-SECTION

Printed onto every one of the six numbered dice below are six letters (one per side), which can be rearranged to form the answer to each clue; however, some sides are invisible to you. Use the clues and write every answer into the grid. When correctly filled, the letters in the shaded squares, reading in the order 1 to 6, will spell out a Dickens character.

1 Bodyguard
2 Hard to please
3 Assassin
4 Move unsteadily
5 Astute
6 Common gas

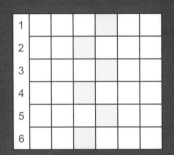

ON TARGET

The answers to the clues read from the outer circle to the center, all ending with the same letter. When you've finished, the letters in the shaded ring will give a word.

1 Limited in size
2 Blacksmith's block
3 Magic formula
4 Tired, timeworn
5 Lawful, licit
6 Perfect

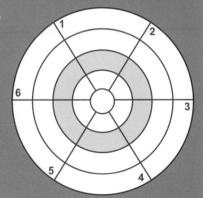

BRAINTEASER

In which year was Ronald Reagan born?

Answers to puzzles on the previous page

Tangled Tackle: Angler A
Movie Quotes: Matt Hooper (Richard Dreyfuss) *Jaws* (1975)
Where on Earth?: Ireland, also Arkansas, Delaware, Ohio, or Pennsylvania, USA

Patchwork:

D	F	B	C	A	E
C	A	D	B	E	F
E	D	A	F	B	C
B	C	E	D	F	A
F	E	C	A	D	B
A	B	F	E	C	D

WHATEVER NEXT?

Which of the numbered alternatives comes next in this sequence:

| A | H | E | L | I | ? |

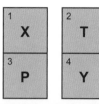

1 X | 2 T
3 P | 4 Y

COUPLINGS

Apart from two, every word listed below can be coupled with one of the others to make another word or phrase. Rearrange the letters of the two which can't be paired together to form one word, a citizen of a certain country.

1 BIG	2 WIND
3 SOME	4 GRASS
5 SHINE	6 HAND
7 GOOSE	8 BANG
9 AIM	10 CUTTER
11 CHIME	12 CRANE
13 MOON	14 FEATHER

Answer: _____

WEATHER for PESSIMISTS

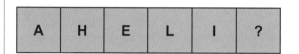

Today the weather will be:

Humid, so that you feel miserable

GET THE LOOK

Make the face:

AMAZED

PICK 'N' MIX

Choose three words to plan your wedding:

Classy   Outlandish
Superior   Canceled
Booze-fest   Chic
Colorblind   Nouvelle
Vogue   Chintz

JIGSAW CROSSWORD

Fit the blocks into the empty grid to form a complete crossword which, when finished, will be symmetrical, similar to the example seen here:

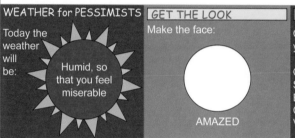

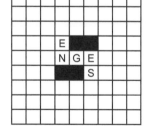

UNLIKELY CANDIDATE

FILM DIRECTOR

_____

Answers to puzzles on the previous page

On Target: 1 Small, 2 Anvil, 3 Spell, 4 Banal, 5 Legal, 6 Ideal.
The word is: AVENGE
Brainteaser: 1911

Dice-Section:

M	I	N	D	E	R
C	H	O	O	S	Y
H	I	T	M	A	N
W	O	B	B	L	E
S	H	R	E	W	D
O	X	Y	G	E	N

13

TODAY'S GREATEST ACHIEVEMENT

Staying calm ☐

Tried new vegetable ☐

Solving the Spacetime Continuum ☐

MASS HYSTERIAS

Today we are all going to:

Climb on the roof and threaten to jump if nobody says anything nice about us.

WHATEVER YOU DO, don't even THINK about…

The theme tune to any of the following:

Titanic
Tom and Jerry
Happy Days
Love Story
Cereal Commercials

BALANCING THE SCALES

Given that scales A and B balance perfectly, how many stars are needed to balance scale C?

WHO AM I?

Bravo! Victim and a dickhead.

I am:

_____

MUSIC TRIVIA

Who had a hit single in 1981 with *Romeo and Juliet*?

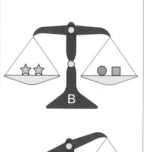

NAMED AND SHAMED

Most likely secret transvestite

_____

Lost the plot

_____

Out in space

_____

PYRAMID PLUS

Every brick in this pyramid contains a number which is the sum of the two numbers below it, so that F=A+B, etc. No two bricks contain the same number, or just a zero, so work out the missing numbers!

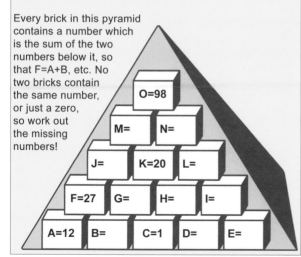

O=98

M=   N=

J=   K=20   L=

F=27   G=   H=   I=

A=12   B=   C=1   D=   E=

STARTING LINE

Which three-letter word can be placed at the start, to form three seven-letter words?

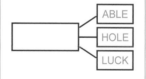

[____] — ABLE
      — HOLE
      — LUCK

Answers to puzzles on the previous page

Whatever Next?:
3 – The letters move forward 7 letters, back 3, forward 7, back 3, etc, so the next in sequence is P.
Couplings: 1/8, 2/11, 4/10, 6/3, 7/14, 13/5.
The letters of 9 and 12 can be rearranged to form AMERICAN.

Jigsaw Crossword:

D	A	T	A		S	H	U	T
A		S		P			E	
M		S	P	E	A	K	E	R
P	A	C	E			I		M
		A	N	G	E	L		
M		L		S	L	A	B	
E	M	P	R	E	S	S		O
S		I		A				W
S	O	U	P		Y	A	W	L

14

MOTHER-IN-LAW VISIT:

1 Play dead

2 Cultivate glassy stare

3 Feign madness…

WAYS TO PASS THE TIME …

Drawing straws ☐

Dancing ☐

Painting walls ☐

WORDFILLER

Can you place all the listed words into the grid below?

3 letters
Bus
Sty

4 letters
Alto
Emit
Magi
Muse

5 letters
Alter
Dukes
Fetid
Flame
Guava
Kebab
Khaki
Ledge
Shawl

Sifts
Staff
Stash
Strew
These
Thief
Tooth
Vexes
Yours

7 letters
Deserve
Digital

9 letters
Laminated

SUDOKU

The numbers from 1 to 9 inclusive need to be placed into the grid below in such a way that every horizontal row and vertical column contains nine different digits. In addition, each of the nine blocks of nine smaller squares should also contain nine different numbers. The clues are the numbers already placed.

7	3					2	1	
4				9		6	8	
			2	7		5		9
	2				1	4		
5	6		3		8		9	1
		7	9				6	
1		8		3	2			
	9	6		8				5
	4	5					7	3

Answers to puzzles on the previous page

Balancing the Scales: 1
Who Am I?: David and Victoria Beckham
Music Trivia: Dire Straits
Pyramid Plus: A=12, B=15, C=1, D=3, E=8, F=27, G=16, H=4, I=11, J=43, K=20, L=15, M=63, N=35, O=98.
Starting Line: POT

JOIN THE DOTS

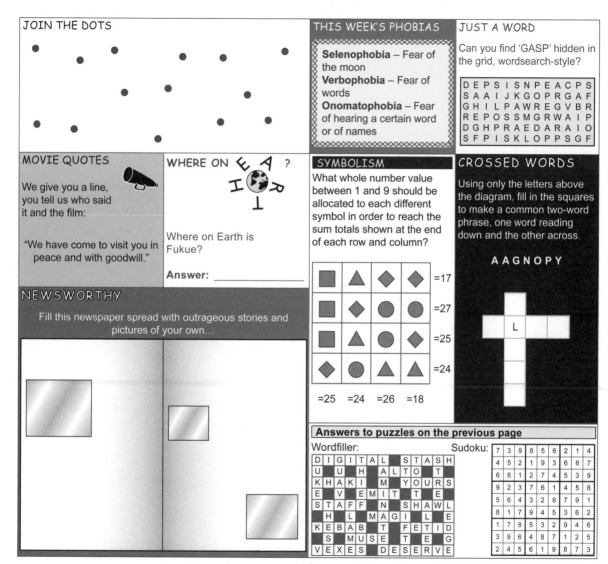

Selenophobia – Fear of the moon

Verbophobia – Fear of words

Onomatophobia – Fear of hearing a certain word or of names

JUST A WORD

Can you find 'GASP' hidden in the grid, wordsearch-style?

```
D E P S I S N P E A C P S
S A A I J K G O P R G A F
G H I L P A W R E G V B R
R E P O S S M G R W A I P
D G H P R A E D A R A I O
S F P I S K L O P P S G F
```

MOVIE QUOTES

We give you a line, you tell us who said it and the film:

"We have come to visit you in peace and with goodwill."

WHERE ON E A R H I T ?

Where on Earth is Fukue?

Answer: _____

SYMBOLISM

What whole number value between 1 and 9 should be allocated to each different symbol in order to reach the sum totals shown at the end of each row and column?

■	▲	◆	◆	=17
■	◆	●	●	=27
■	▲	●	◆	=25
◆	●	▲	▲	=24
=25	=24	=26	=18	

CROSSED WORDS

Using only the letters above the diagram, fill in the squares to make a common two-word phrase, one word reading down and the other across.

A A G N O P Y

(cross grid with L in center)

NEWSWORTHY

Fill this newspaper spread with outrageous stories and pictures of your own…

OUT OF PLACE

Two letters have already been placed in this grid; your job is to replace the remaining 18 to create four words reading across and five words reading down. To make things slightly easier, each letter must be placed in the row or column against which it appears; thus the first A must go in the first column and the first L must go in the top row. Good luck; beware of false starts!

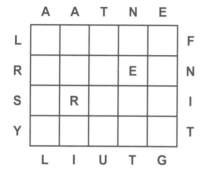

```
        A   A   T   N   E
   L  [                 ]  F
   R  [          E      ]  N
   S  [     R           ]  I
   Y  [                 ]  T
        L   I   U   T   G
```

BRAINTEASER

In which year did Pablo Picasso die?

TWO DOWN

Fit five of the seven listed words into the Across rows in the grid, so that the other two words read down the shaded columns numbered 2 and 3.

AVERT   CORGI
DEPOT   FLUID
HEDGE   REVEL
TRUCE

```
| 1 | 2 |   | 3 |   |
| 4 |   |   |   |   |
| 5 |   |   |   |   |
| 6 |   |   |   |   |
| 7 |   |   |   |   |
```

NUMB-SKULL

Fit the listed numbers into the grid, crossword-fashion.

3 digits	5 digits
347	25561
400	42404
529	43296
712	43653
	57297
4 digits	64161
1254	87340
1436	93753
1766	
1937	**7 digits**
2174	1870610
3173	5318951
3563	
6368	
6981	
8874	
9512	
9571	

MUSIC TRIVIA

Which British female singer had a 2006 hit with *Rehab*?

amy Winehouse

BOX CLEVER

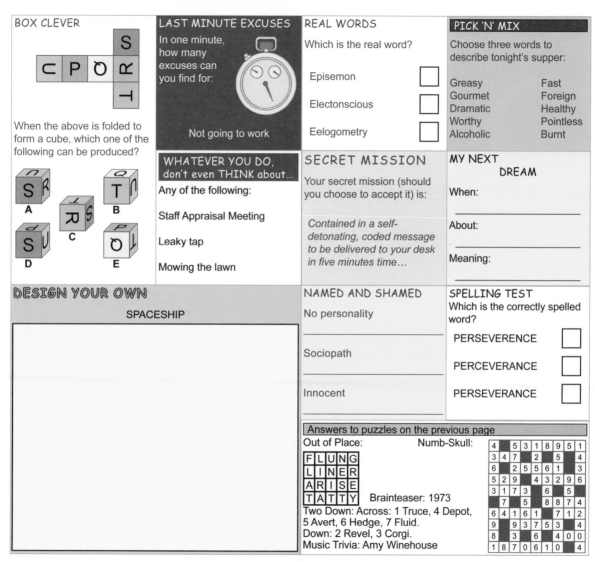

S
C U P O R
T

When the above is folded to form a cube, which one of the following can be produced?

A S R / U
B T Q / N
C T / R S
D S U / d
E P / O t

LAST MINUTE EXCUSES

In one minute, how many excuses can you find for:

Not going to work

WHATEVER YOU DO, don't even THINK about...

Any of the following:

Staff Appraisal Meeting

Leaky tap

Mowing the lawn

REAL WORDS

Which is the real word?

Episemon ☐

Electonscious ☐

Eelogometry ☐

SECRET MISSION

Your secret mission (should you choose to accept it) is:

Contained in a self-detonating, coded message to be delivered to your desk in five minutes time...

PICK 'N' MIX

Choose three words to describe tonight's supper:

Greasy   Fast
Gourmet   Foreign
Dramatic   Healthy
Worthy   Pointless
Alcoholic   Burnt

MY NEXT DREAM

When:
_____

About:
_____

Meaning:
_____

DESIGN YOUR OWN

SPACESHIP

NAMED AND SHAMED

No personality
_____

Sociopath
_____

Innocent
_____

SPELLING TEST

Which is the correctly spelled word?

PERSEVERENCE ☐

PERCEVERANCE ☐

PERSEVERANCE ☐

Answers to puzzles on the previous page

Out of Place:

F L U N G
L I N E R
A R I S E
T A T T Y

Numb-Skull:

4		5	3	1	8	9	5	1
3	4	7		2		5		4
6		2	5	5	6	1		3
5	2	9		4	3	2	9	6
3	1	7	3		6		5	
	7		5		8	8	7	4
6	4	1	6	1		7	1	2
9		9	3	7	5	3		4
8		3		6		4	0	0
1	8	7	0	6	1	0		4

Brainteaser: 1973

Two Down: Across: 1 Truce, 4 Depot, 5 Avert, 6 Hedge, 7 Fluid.
Down: 2 Revel, 3 Corgi.

Music Trivia: Amy Winehouse

Simply fill in the letters missing from the different words numbered 1-6 and enter them into the numbered boxes, to reveal the hidden keyword. Take care, however, as some may have more than one possible letter which could fit: for example S — M E might be either SAME or SOME.

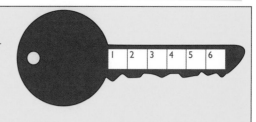

| 1 | 2 | 3 | 4 | 5 | 6 |

1 —URKY

2 GR—NT

3 CA—P

4 K—TE

5 ROU—DEL

6 FR—AK

WORDSEARCH

Can you find all of the listed words relating to fun and games in the grid? Words may run in either a forwards or backwards direction, horizontally, vertically or diagonally, but always in a straight, uninterrupted line.

BASEBALL

BOATING

BOWLS

CANOE

DARTS

HAMMER

HOCKEY

HURDLES

LACROSSE

LOTTO

LUDO

OLYMPICS

POOL

RELAY

ROWING

```
B O A T I N G P C H P Z G
H T D T S L W O B O D N D
M U U U H P I O G C I Q P
E S R G L U O L Q K R Y Y
N H O D O N W R L E Q S Y
I U W H L F I A T Y O A A
L T I D Y E W R D C L B C
O T N E M M S A C E A W H
P L G O P Q I E R S K A T
M E T N I T R B E C M C O
A C Z A C D R B A M T G O
R O W C S B A R E E M T K
T C V P U L T R C W T S U
Q K C V L W T J T O U J N
E S S O R C A L L S X I O
```

SHUTTLECOCK

SOCCER

SPORT

TRACK

TRAMPOLINE

TUG OF WAR

WALKING

YACHT

TOP FIVE

Best songs for a wedding:

1 _____

_____

2 _____

_____

3 _____

_____

4 _____

_____

5 _____

_____

SWEET BAD MUSIC

So who on earth was responsible for this lyric?

"I love you like
A fat kid love cake"

Answers to puzzles on the previous page

Box Clever: D
Real Words: Episemon
Spelling Test: PERSEVERANCE

19

SIMPLE AS A,B,C

In the grid, each row across, column down and diagonal line of six squares should contain two each of A, B and C. The clues relate to the squares only in that row or column. We give as many clues as we think you need (including any letters already in the grid), so can you place the letters correctly?

Across:
2 Any three adjacent squares contain three different letters.
3 The As are further left than the Bs.
4 The As are between the Bs.
5 The As are between the Cs.
6 The Cs are between the Bs.

Down:
1 The Cs are between the Bs.
2 The As are between the Cs.
3 The As are between the Cs.
4 The Cs are between the As.
5 The As are lower than the Cs.
6 The Cs are between the As.

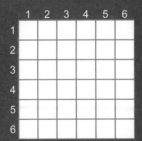

WORD LADDER

Change one letter at a time (but not the position of any letter) to make a new word – and move from the word at the top of the ladder to the word at the bottom using the exact number of rungs provided.

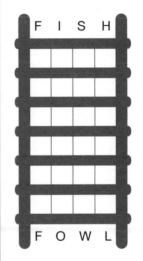

GOOD IMPRESSIONS

Can you pair up these door keys with the impressions of their ends?

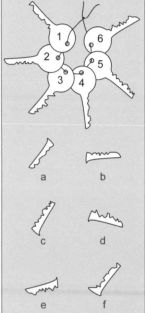

PRE-FAME NAME GAME

By what name do we know this famous person?

Thomas John Woodward

ALL AT SEA

What was the name of Captain Nemo's submarine?

20

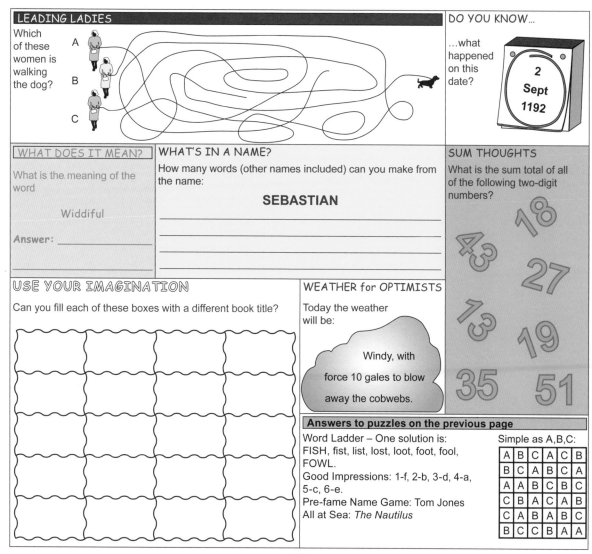

LEADING LADIES

Which of these women is walking the dog?

A

B

C

DO YOU KNOW...

...what happened on this date?

2 Sept 1192

WHAT DOES IT MEAN?

What is the meaning of the word

Widdiful

Answer: _____

WHAT'S IN A NAME?

How many words (other names included) can you make from the name:

SEBASTIAN

_____
_____
_____
_____

SUM THOUGHTS

What is the sum total of all of the following two-digit numbers?

18

43

27

13

19

35   51

USE YOUR IMAGINATION

Can you fill each of these boxes with a different book title?

WEATHER for OPTIMISTS

Today the weather will be:

Windy, with force 10 gales to blow away the cobwebs.

Answers to puzzles on the previous page

Word Ladder – One solution is:
FISH, fist, list, lost, loot, foot, fool, FOWL.
Good Impressions: 1-f, 2-b, 3-d, 4-a, 5-c, 6-e.
Pre-fame Name Game: Tom Jones
All at Sea: *The Nautilus*

Simple as A,B,C:

A	B	C	A	C	B
B	C	A	B	C	A
A	A	B	C	B	C
C	B	A	C	A	B
C	A	B	A	B	C
B	C	C	B	A	A

ON THE TILES

In this puzzle, the eight tiles on the right must be fitted into the pattern in the middle so as to form four words reading across and five words reading down. No tile may be rotated!

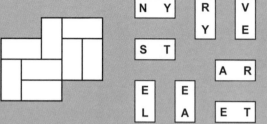

Today the weather will be:

Pleasant and sunny enough to know it won't last

AMAZING

Can you work your way from the entrance at the top to the exit at the bottom of this maze?

ROUNDWORD

Write the answer to each clue in a clockwise direction. Every solution overlaps the next by either one, two or three letters and each solution starts in its numbered section.
The solution to the final clue ends with the letter in the first square.

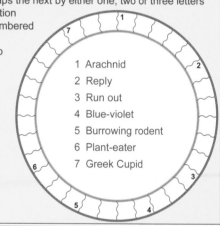

1 Arachnid
2 Reply
3 Run out
4 Blue-violet
5 Burrowing rodent
6 Plant-eater
7 Greek Cupid

Answers to puzzles on the previous page

Leading Ladies: Woman C
Do You Know…: Sultan Saladin and King Richard the Lionheart signed an agreement ending the third crusade.
What Does It Mean?: Someone who deserves to be hanged.
Sum Thoughts: 206

22

TOP FIVE

Best clothes:

1 _____
2 _____
3 _____
4 _____
5 _____

STARTING LINE

Which three-letter word can be placed at the start, to form three seven-letter words?

```
┌─────────┐   ┌──────┐
│         │───│ BAGS │
│         │   └──────┘
│         │   ┌──────┐
│         │───│ TIME │
│         │   └──────┘
│         │   ┌──────┐
│         │───│ WEED │
└─────────┘   └──────┘
```

MUSIC TRIVIA

Which Barbadian singer had a massive No 1 hit with *Umbrella*?

GET THE LOOK

Make the face:

DISCOMBOBULATED

IN CHAINS

This chain of letters contains the names of three animals. The letters are in the correct order but need to be picked out.

CSLKAIUMNOEKNL

_____   _____

_____

CROSSWISE

Rearrange the six scrambled groups of letters to form words and then decide where each fits in the grid. Some letters are already in place.

ACENNU   AEEGGR
AGRSUY   CEPRSU
GINOPS   IRPSTU

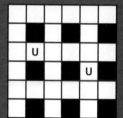

WHOLESOME FUN

In this puzzle, you need to find a five-letter word by deciding which common letter has been removed from the trios of words on each line.
Enter that letter into the circle at the end of each row and the word will be revealed reading downwards.

WA_E	THU_	_OLD	◯
REA_	_IFE	LO_E	◯
_ASE	DU_T	LIM_	◯
S_AR	SLO_	PO_T	◯
MOO_	_AIL	PI_E	◯

LAST MINUTE EXCUSES

In one minute, how many excuses can you find for:

Not washing

Answers to puzzles on the previous page

On the Tiles:

```
      V E T
S T E E R
E A R L Y
A N Y
```

Roundword: 1 Spider, 2 Respond, 3 Drain, 4 Indigo, 5 Gopher, 6 Herbivore, 7 Eros.

Amazing:

TOP TEN

CUPS ☐

SAUCERS ☐

PANS ☐

KETTLES ☐

PLATES ☐

JUGS ☐

TRAYS ☐

BOWLS ☐

GLASSES ☐

BAKING TRAYS ☐

SPOT THE SAME

Only two of these modern abstract paintings are identical in every way: which?

NUMBER BOX

In this puzzle, simply use the hints given to enter nine different numbers 1-9 in their correct boxes.

2 is two squares above 8
8 is next to and right of 6
6 is further left than 7
1 is between 5 and 7
5 is next to and above 3
3 is two squares below 4
9 is not in the middle square

THE NAME GAME

Can you complete the six words reading across in such a way as to reveal the name of a well-known person in the shaded columns?

	E	A		S
	C	R		D
	O	U		D
	R	A		E
	A	D		N
	I	A		Y

ON TARGET

The answers to the clues read from the outer circle to the center, all ending with the same letter. When you've finished, the letters in the shaded ring will give a word.

1 French river and World War I battle

2 Nimble

3 Taut, uneasy

4 Scoundrel

5 Untrue

6 Greek island

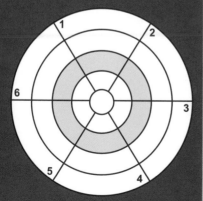

NIGHT ANIMALS

What type of animal lives in a sett?

Answers to puzzles on the previous page

Starting Line: RAG
Music Trivia: Rihanna
In Chains: Camel, Skunk and Lion
Wholesome Fun: GREEN

Crosswise:

P	U	R	I	S	T
O		E		P	
S	U	G	A	R	Y
I		G		U	
N	U	A	N	C	E
G		E		E	

24

PARTNERS IN RHYME

Each of the pairs below is a rhyme for a familiar phrase. Can you identify them?

1. Ear and brow _____

2. Star and bride _____

3. Wok and bowl _____

4. Rack and rue _____

UNFINISHED PICTURE

Can you complete this doodle?

QUOTE OF THE DAY

"How many legs does a dog have if you call the tail a leg? Four. Calling a tail a leg doesn't make it a leg."

Abraham Lincoln

UNLIKELY CANDIDATE

PRIEST

_____

DO YOU KNOW...

...what happened in Mexico on this date?

23 August 1821

JIGSAW CROSSWORD

Fit the blocks into the empty grid to form a complete crossword which, when finished, will be symmetrical, similar to the example seen here:

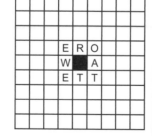

NAMED AND SHAMED

Hopeless worker

_____

Secret government spy

_____

Most likely to cry

_____

Answers to puzzles on the previous page

Spot the Same: D and E

The Name Game:
Heaps, Acrid, Round, Orate, Laden, Diary.
Person: Harold Pinter

On Target: 1 Somme, 2 Agile, 3 Tense, 4 Rogue, 5 False, 6 Crete.

The word is: MINGLE

Night Animals: Badger

Number Box:

4	9	2
5	1	7
3	6	8

25

MOVIE QUOTES

We give you a line,  you tell us who said it and the film:

"The question is not whether I've treated you rudely but whether you've ever heard me treat anyone else better."

WHERE ON EARTH?

Where on Earth is Cunter?

Answer: _____

TODAY'S GREATEST ACHIEVEMENT

Washing up ☐

Buying bread ☐

Being elected president ☐

IN SHAPE

How many circles can you see here?

GET THE LOOK

Make the face:

DAZED

DOMINOLOGICAL

What is the value of the question mark?

PYRAMID PLUS

Every brick in this pyramid contains a number which is the sum of the two numbers below it, so that F=A+B, etc. No two bricks contain the same number, or just a zero, so work out the missing numbers!

O=88

M= N=48

J= K=19 L=

F= G=8 H= I=

A= B=3 C= D= E=

WHO AM I?

He's grown large 'n' crazed

I am:

_____

LETTER TRACKER

Begin in the central shaded square and follow a continuous path which will track from square to square, up, down and sideways, but never diagonally.

Your trail should cover every letter once only, in order to find:

Fourteen cheeses.

M	A	C	E	M	M	E	G	R	J	T
E	H	I	R	E	N	T	B	E	A	R
M	S	R	O	G	L	A	S	L	R	O
B	E	G	O	Y	D	A	L	O	Q	F
E	H	C	N	E	L	S	E	R	U	E
R	T	E	Z	O	M	N	E	W	A	L
T	T	D	A	L	A	Z	A	R	E	L
C	A	O	L	S	R	Z	O	M	I	L
H	L	E	C	C	A	R	P	E	T	S
E	A	R	R	M	A	N	O	N	A	I
D	D	P	A	E	S	G	O	U	D	T

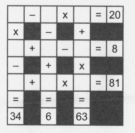

ELIMINATION

Every oval shape contains a different letter from A to K inclusive. Use the clues to determine their locations. Reference in the clues to 'due' means in any location along the same horizontal or vertical line.

1   E is due west of B and due south of C.

2   A is due west of F and due north of (and next to) H.

3   J is due north of D, which is due north of G, which is due west of K.

4   I is due south of E, which is further north than A.

5   C is further east than J.

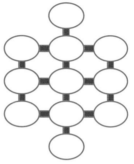

TWO-WORD HOROSCOPES

Aries – lost again?

Taurus – dirty dog

Gemini – not now!

Cancer – so what?

Leo – keep quiet

Virgo – forever lost

Libra – good timing

Scorpio – idiotic capers

Sagittarius – scary times

Capricorn – go on!

Aquarius – well done!

Pisces – could you?

DESIGN YOUR OWN

BOUDOIR

MY NEXT DATE

Who:
_____

Where:
_____

Result:
_____

Answers to puzzles on the previous page

What Does It Mean?: The abuse of military power or authority

Brainteaser: 1900

Letter Tracker: Marscarpone, Mozzarella, Wensleydale, Roquefort, Jarlsberg, Emmental, Gorgonzola, Dolcelatte, Cheshire, Camembert, Cheddar, Parmesan, Gouda, Tilsit.

Sum Total:

7	–	2	x	4
x		–		+
6	+	5	–	3
–		+		x
8	+	1	x	9

TOTAL CONCENTRATION

Can you fill in the missing numbers so that each row, each column and two longest diagonal lines meet the totals given?

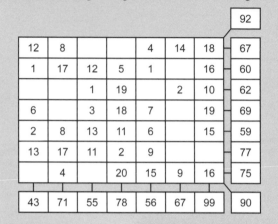

							92
12	8			4	14	18	67
1	17	12	5	1		16	60
		1	19		2	10	62
6		3	18	7		19	69
2	8	13	11	6		15	59
13	17	11	2	9			77
	4		20	15	9	16	75
43	71	55	78	56	67	99	90

WORD LADDER

Change one letter at a time (but not the position of any letter) to make a new word – and move from the word at the top of the ladder to the word at the bottom using the exact number of rungs provided.

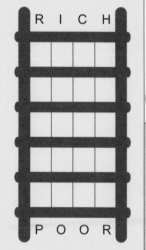

R I C H

P O O R

STARTING LINE

Which three-letter word can be placed at the start, to form three seven-letter words?

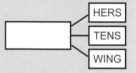

HERS

TENS

WING

WEATHER for OPTIMISTS

Today the weather will be:

Grey and dull. You can wear your brightest clothes and stand out in a crowd.

TIED UP AT PRESENT

Which boy is holding the string attached to the present?

A B C

TWO DOWN

Fit five of the seven listed words into the Across rows in the grid, so that the other two words read down the shaded columns numbered 2 and 3.

APART   AWARE
FROWN   GRAPE
NOMAD   OFFAL
UNITY

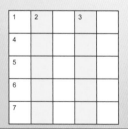

1	2		3	
4				
5				
6				
7				

PICK 'N' MIX

Choose three words to describe your fashion look:

Bonkers   Regurgitated
Ethnic   Eco
Classic   Abstract
Colorful   Uber-...
Puritan   Secondhand

Answers to puzzles on the previous page

Elimination:

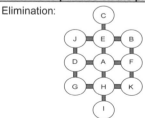

29

CLOCKWORDS

It's a race against the clock… How many common words of three or more different letters can you make from those on the clock face (without using plurals, proper nouns or abbreviations) in ten minutes? All words must contain BOTH the letters indicated by the hands on the clock.

QUOTE OF THE DAY

"There are some sluggish men who are improved by drinking; as there are fruits that are not good until they are rotten."

Samuel Johnson

WEATHER for PESSIMISTS

Today the weather will be:

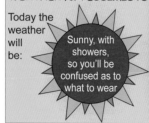

Sunny, with showers, so you'll be confused as to what to wear

DICEY ARITHMETIC

Using three of the arithmetical signs ÷, −, x and +, can you achieve the correct total?

BERMUDA TRIANGLE

Travel through the 'Bermuda Triangle' by visiting one room at a time and collecting a letter from each. You can enter the outside passageway as often as you like, but can only visit each room once. When you've completed your tour, the 15 letters spell out a word.

PROVERBS AND SAYINGS

The letters on the tiles were once all in place, but dropped out, falling in a straight line into the lower grid. Some tiles dropped earlier than others, so those on the lowest row aren't all from the same row in the grid above. Can you put them back into position in order to reveal a well-known proverb or saying?

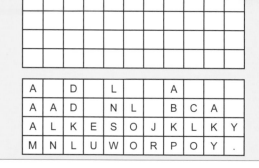

A		D		L			A		
A	A	D		N	L		B	C	A
A	L	K	E	S	O	J	K	L	K	Y
M	N	L	U	W	O	R	P	O	Y	.

JOIN THE DOTS

MISSING LINKS

Which word links the one on the left with the one on the right? We've done the first one, and when you've finished them all, the first letters of the link words will spell another word.

WHIPPING	**BOY**	FRIEND
PRIM		WOOD
WORN		SIDE
FIRE		STREET
FORT		MARE

MUSIC TRIVIA

Which singer had a string of hits in the 1970s and is often referred to as the Queen of Disco?

LETTER TRACKER

Begin in the central shaded square and follow a continuous path which will track from square to square, up, down and sideways, but never diagonally.

Your trail should cover every letter once only, in order to find:

Seventeen items of clothing and headgear.

U	M	S	O	H	C	T	A	W	I	R
F	F	T	R	S	O	S	I	E	H	T
E	L	I	N	T	A	F	O	R	S	S
R	C	K	G	L	I	A	N	I	R	C
R	A	C	S	G	G	E	E	P	E	A
D	I	O	N	E	M	L	L	O	V	R
T	G	T	T	T	I	U	L	B	U	F
I	A	S	E	R	E	P	E	T	O	D
U	N	S	N	A	E	S	E	F	A	J
S	D	U	N	G	A	E	D	O	R	A
M	I	W	S	S	N	J	T	E	K	C

SWEET BAD MUSIC

So who on earth was responsible for this lyric?

"There's an insect
In your ear
If you scratch
It won't disappear"

MISSING LETTERS

One letter of the alphabet is missing from each box. Find them all and place them in the order of the numbered boxes to reveal a six-letter word.

Word: _____

1	2	3
EKAPD	ZQJBF	JKQAD
TJBOF	EVNAD	TEMZG
ZNGXS	UGYPK	PXNBF
HCWRL	LTXHC	YHOCL
YUVQI	RWSMI	IVWUS

4	5	6
VEPAD	XERZD	ONAKD
BZKMF	SBWOF	RYUBF
WLGSJ	YTGPN	ZMPIG
HUOCX	JKMHC	HTXEC
QNIYR	LUQIV	WVQJS

Answers to puzzles on the previous page

Dicey Arithmetic: The signs are ÷, + and −.
Bermuda Triangle: THOUGHTLESSNESS
Proverbs and Sayings: All work and no play makes Jack a dull boy.

BOX CLEVER

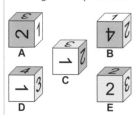

When the above is folded to form a cube, which one of the following can be produced?

A
B
C
D
E

WORDWHEEL

Using only the letters in the Wordwheel, you have ten minutes to find as many words as possible, none of which may be plurals, foreign words or proper nouns. Each word must be of three letters or more, all must contain the central letter and letters can only be used once in every word. There is at least one nine-letter word in the wheel.

Nine-letter word: _____

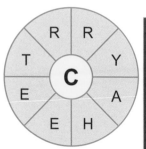

LAST MINUTE EXCUSES

In one minute, how many excuses can you find for:

Drinking lots of beer

TOP TEN

CHARACTER ASSIGNATION

Fill in the answers to the clues, across the grid. Then read down the diagonal line of seven squares, to reveal:
A character from Charles Dickens' *A Christmas Carol*.

1 Brutal
2 Still
3 Singing group
4 Nothing
5 Menagerie
6 'For example' abbreviated
7 Letter at 'three o'clock' on a compass

CHARACTER: _____

WHATEVER YOU DO, don't even THINK about...

Bad things you did at school

Bad things you did at work

Bad things you did last night

SPELLING TEST

Which is the correctly spelled word?

SEPARATELY ☐

SEPERATELY ☐

SEPERATLY ☐

Answers to puzzles on the previous page

Missing Links: Boy, Rose, Out, Wall, Night. Thus: BROWN
Music Trivia: Donna Summer
Letter Tracker: Mittens, Stockings, Negligee, Pinafore, Waistcoat, Shorts, Muffler, Cardigan, Dungarees, Pullover, Shirt, Scarf, Doublet, Fedora, Jacket, Jeans, Swimsuit.
Sweet Bad Music: U2 *Staring at the Sun*
Missing Letters: MORTAL

BROKEN-HEARTED

Don't be halfhearted in your attempts to get these couples back together again! Match both sides of each heart, to reveal their names.

_____ & _____   _____ & _____   _____ & _____
_____ & _____   _____ & _____   _____ & _____

CHA LYN — A

HUR DRA — B

NIS IAM — C

LIAM THA — D

ART SAN — E

DEN MIR — F

DON ELA — G

GOR PAM — H

WIL BER — I

RLES DA — J

PET JE — K

ER NNY — L

EGG TIMER

Can you complete this puzzle in the time it takes to boil an egg? The answers to the clues are anagrams of the words immediately above and below, plus or minus a letter.

1 Contended
2 Pill
3 Sheep's call
4 Tardy
5 Fastener, fixing
6 Red Bordeaux wine
7 Bright red

WAYS TO PASS THE TIME ...

Racing beetles ☐

Crawling ☐

Rolling over and over ☐

ODD ONE OUT

Which one is different to the rest?

A   B

C   D

E   F

TODAY'S GREATEST ACHIEVEMENT

Being polite to your boss ☐

Having a liquid lunch ☐

Saving someone's life ☐

MASS HYSTERIAS

Today we are all going to:

Draw smiley faces on everybody's car windshield.

Answers to puzzles on the previous page

Box Clever: D
Wordwheel: The nine-letter word is TREACHERY
Character Assignation: 1 Vicious, 2 Static, 3 Choir, 4 Zero, 5 Zoo, 6 Eg, 7 E.
Character: Scrooge.
Spelling Test: SEPARATELY

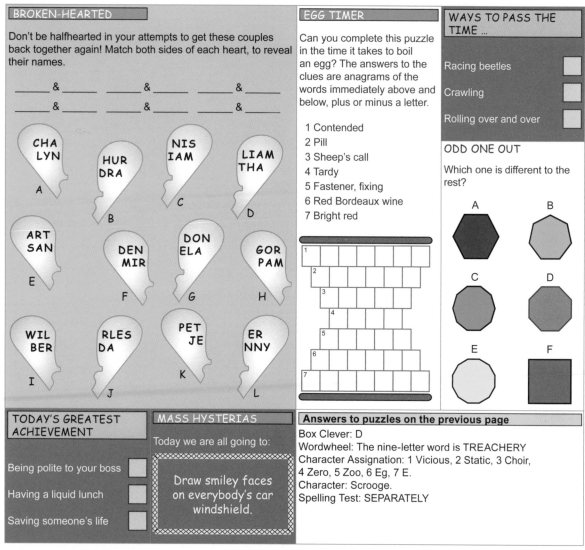

ON THE TILES

In this puzzle, the eight tiles on the right must be fitted into the pattern in the middle so as to form four words reading across and five words reading down. No tile may be rotated!

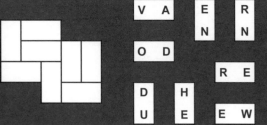

LOOSE VOWELS

Someone has taken all the vowels out of what was once a completed crossword. Can you put them all back in again? You should use only those letters beneath the grid.

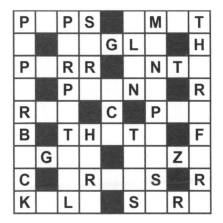

A A A A A A A
E E E E E E E E E E E E E
I I I I I
O O O O
U U U U U

A MATCHING PAIR

Which are the only two mugs that are identical in every way?

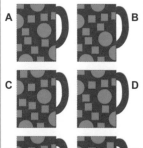

A   B

C   D

E   F

Answers to puzzles on the previous page

Broken-hearted: A and J, E and B, F and C, H and G, I and D, K and L.

Egg Timer: 1 Battled, 2 Tablet, 3 Bleat, 4 Late, 5 Cleat, 6 Claret, 7 Scarlet.

Odd One Out: B – It has an odd number of sides.

DESIGN YOUR OWN
BEACH BAR

PAIR SHAPES
In the box below there are shapes in three different colors, red, white and blue. Any shape may have been rotated, but can you see which is the only shape to appear exactly twice in exactly the same color?

REAL WORDS
Which is the real word?

Funogometry ☐

Funototality ☐

Famulus ☐

STARTER LETTER
Write down one each of the listed items, all of which must begin with the starter letter:

R

Country	
Tree	
Boy's name	
Girl's name	
River	
City	
Animal	
Make of car	
Drink	

CROSSED WORDS
Using only the letters above the diagram, fill in the squares to make a common two-word phrase, one word reading down and the other across.

B E E L M R S

PRE-FAME NAME GAME
By what name do we know this famous person?

Joe Yule, Jr

BRAINTEASER
What was Muhammad Ali's birth name?

Answers to puzzles on the previous page
On the Tiles:

H	E	W		
E	V	A	D	E
R	E	R	U	N
		N	O	D

Loose Vowels:

P	U	P	S		E	M	I	T
A		E	A	G	L	E		H
P	U	R	R		A	N	T	E
E		P	I	A	N	O		R
R	U	E		C		P	I	E
B		T	H	E	T	A		F
A	G	U	E		O	U	Z	O
C		A	R	I	E	S		R
K	I	L	O		S	E	R	E

A Matching Pair: A and D

35

CODEWORD

This is a crossword puzzle in code. Every number represents a different letter of the alphabet and this number remains the same throughout the puzzle. Use the letters either side of the grid as well as the check-box below the grid to keep a track on your progress.

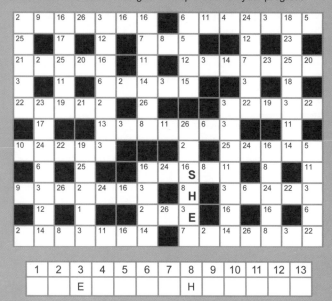

1	2	3	4	5	6	7	8	9	10	11	12	13
		E					H					

14	15	16	17	18	19	20	21	22	23	24	25	26
		S										

BRIEF SURVIVAL GUIDE

JOB INTERVIEWS:

1 Confidence

2 Silence

3 Stay in bed

A IS TO B

A is to B

as C is to

D   E

F   G

ARRANGING THINGS

If you fit six of these seven words into the grid, the word left over will appear reading down the shaded squares.

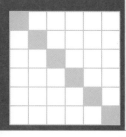

AKIMBO   ANYONE
FIDDLE   FRIEND
FRISKY   SECOND
    SPEECH

Answers to puzzles on the previous page

Pair Shapes: ∏
Real Words: ∐
Famulus
Crossed Words: Laser beam
Pre-fame Name Game: Mickey Rooney
Brainteaser: Cassius Clay

EYE-SPY

I spy with my little eye
something beginning with:

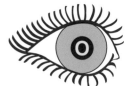

_____

MIRROR WRITING

Write this word upside down:

BREACH

_____

DO YOU KNOW...

...what was launched in Florida on this date?

31 January 1958

WHAT DOES IT MEAN?

What is the meaning of the word

Lamprophony

Answer: _____

_____

COMPLETE THIS LIMERICK:

There was a young man from Peru

Whose eyelashes just grew and grew

When he winked at a girl

She'd go into a whirl

_____

SWEET BAD MUSIC

So who on earth was responsible for this lyric?

"Relentless lust
Of rotting flesh
To thrash the tomb she lies
Heathen whore
Of Satan's wrath
I spit at your demise"

DOMINADDITION

Can you place the remaining dominoes in their correct positions, so that the total number of spots in each of the four rows and five columns equals the sum at the end of that row or column?

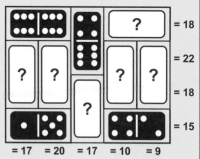

= 18
= 22
= 18
= 15

= 17   = 20   = 17   = 10   = 9

WHO AM I?

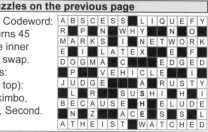

Mr Jawbones

I am:

_____

Answers to puzzles on the previous page

A is to B: Codeword:

F – The whole turns 45 degrees, and the inner and outer colors swap.

Arranging Things:
Across (from the top):
Fiddle, Frisky, Akimbo, Speech, Anyone, Second.
Down: Friend.

A	B	S	C	E	S	S		L	I	Q	U	E	F	Y
R		P		N		W	H	Y		N		O		
M	A	R	K	S		I		N	E	T	W	O	R	K
E		I		L	A	T	E	X			E		F	
D	O	G	M	A		C			E	D	G	E	D	
	P			V	E	H	I	C	L	E			I	
J	U	D	G	E				A		R	U	S	T	Y
	L		R			S	U	S	H	I		H		I
B	E	C	A	U	S	E		H		E	L	U	D	E
	N		Z			A	C	E		S		S		L
A	T	H	E	I	S	T		W	A	T	C	H	E	D

37

THE NAME GAME

Can you complete the six words reading across in such a way as to reveal the name of a well-known person in the shaded columns?

O	K		N
A	N		Y
R	B		T
I	D		T
L	L		Y
C	E		E

SHAPE RECOGNITION

Which are the only three pieces which will fit together to form a copy of this black shape?

REAL WORDS

Which is the real word?

Frigorific ☐

Frigormornian ☐

Frigodasian ☐

CELEBRITY WRESTLING

VANNA WHITE

-v-

SARAH PALIN

HEXAGONY

Can you place the hexagons in the grid, so that where any triangle touches another along a straight line, the contents of both are the same? One triangle is already filled.

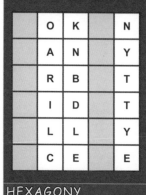

PRE-FAME NAME GAME

By what name do we know this famous person?

Michael Shalhoub

_____

MUSIC TRIVIA

Which boy's name was the title of the debut album released by Amy Winehouse?

Answers to puzzles on the previous page

Do You Know…: The first US satellite, *Explorer 1*, from Cape Canaveral.
What Does It Mean?: Loudness and clarity of voice.
Sweet Bad Music: Slayer *Necrophiliac*
Who Am I?: James Brown

Dominaddition:

6	6	4	1	1
5	3	6	2	6
5	6	4	3	0
1	5	3	4	2

SNAKES AND LADDERS

This is a standard game, so when you land at the foot of a ladder, you climb it; and when you land on the head of a snake, you slide down its tail. You need to throw an exact number to land on 100 to win – counting backwards if you don't, eg if you land on 98 and throw a five, you will end up on 97. The dice is thrown for you and always lands in this recurring order: 1, 6, 4, 2, 3, 5, so you can start by immediately placing your counter on square 1. Good luck – hope you win!

100	99	98	97	96	95	94	93	92	91
81	82	83	84	85	86	87	88	89	90
80	79	78	77	76	75	74	73	72	71
61	62	63	64	65	66	67	68	69	70
60	59	58	57	56	55	54	53	52	51
41	42	43	44	45	46	47	48	49	50
40	39	38	37	36	35	34	33	32	31
21	22	23	24	25	26	27	28	29	30
20	19	18	17	16	15	14	13	12	11
1	2	3	4	5	6	7	8	9	10

TANGLED TACKLE

Which of these anglers has landed the fish?

A   B   C

PATCHWORK

Fit the letters A, B, C, D, E and F into the grid below, so that every horizontal row, every vertical column and every shape of six smaller squares contain six different letters. Some are already in place.

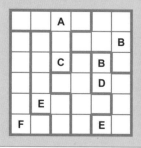

WHO AM I?

It's nasal, tiresome

I am:

_____

WHERE ON EARTH?

Where on Earth is Dyckesville?

Answer: _____

QUOTE OF THE DAY

"A good novel tells us the truth about its hero; but a bad novel tells us the truth about its author."

G K Chesterton

Answers to puzzles on the previous page

The Name Game:
Token, Handy, Orbit, Midst, Alloy, Scene.
Person: Thomas Edison
Shape Recognition:
B, G and H
Real Words: Frigorific
Pre-fame Name Game: Omar Sharif
Music Trivia: Frank

Hexagony:

DICE-SECTION

Printed onto every one of the six numbered dice below are six letters (one per side), which can be rearranged to form the answer to each clue; however, some sides are invisible to you. Use the clues and write every answer into the grid. When correctly filled, the letters in the shaded squares, reading in the order 1 to 6, will spell out the name of a country.

1 Constellation and zodiacal sign

2 Confectionery item

3 Roman ruler

4 Missing

5 Salty

6 Mythological creature

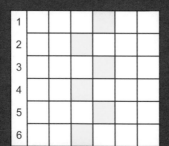

TOP TEN

GIN

WHISKY

VODKA

WINE

BEER

LAGER

VERMOUTH

TEQUILA

PORT

SHERRY

ON TARGET

The answers to the clues read from the outer circle to the center, all ending with the same letter. When you've finished, the letters in the shaded ring will give a word.

1 Spicy dish

2 Mad

3 Currency

4 Unusually small person

5 Question

6 Apologetic, rueful

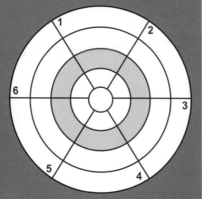

PRE-FAME NAME GAME

By what name do we know this famous person?

Georgios Panayiotou

Answers to puzzles on the previous page

Tangled Tackle: Angler C
Who Am I?: Alanis Morissette
Where on Earth?: Wisconsin, USA

Patchwork:

B	D	A	F	C	E
D	C	E	A	F	B
A	F	C	E	B	D
E	A	F	B	D	C
C	E	B	D	A	F
F	B	D	C	E	A

WHATEVER NEXT?

Which of the numbered alternatives comes next in this sequence:

| H | J | I | L | K | ? |

| 1 H | 2 O |
| 3 A | 4 V |

COUPLINGS

Apart from two, every word listed below can be coupled with one of the others to make another word or phrase. Rearrange the letters of the two which can't be paired together to form one word, the name of an outdoor activity.

1 SHIP	2 FIELD
3 SHAFT	4 FORE
5 FLOOR	6 OCEAN
7 CORN	8 COURT
9 GLAD	10 RASP
11 BERRY	12 FRIEND
13 CRANK	14 PAIRING

Answer: _____

WEATHER for PESSIMISTS

Today the weather will be:

Miserable enough to make life not worth living

GET THE LOOK

Make the face:

ANXIOUS

PICK 'N' MIX

Choose three words to describe your home:

Elegant — Stylish
Dirty — Bohemian
Immaculate — Scruffy
Cheap — Luxurious
Comfortable — Noisy

UNLIKELY CANDIDATE

FILM STAR

_____

JIGSAW CROSSWORD

Fit the blocks into the empty grid to form a complete crossword which, when finished, will be symmetrical, similar to the example seen here:

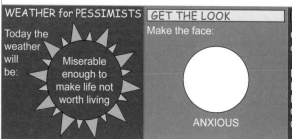

| Answers to puzzles on the previous page |

On Target: 1 Curry, 2 Crazy, 3 Money, 4 Pygmy, 5 Query, 6 Sorry.
The word is: RANGER
Pre-fame Name Game: George Michael

Dice-Section:

T	A	U	R	U	S
N	O	U	G	A	T
C	A	E	S	A	R
A	B	S	E	N	T
S	A	L	I	N	E
D	R	A	G	O	N

MOVIE QUOTES

We give you a line, you tell us who said it and the film:

"Oxygen gets you high. In a catastrophic emergency, you're taking giant panicked breaths. Suddenly you become euphoric, docile. You accept your fate. It's all right here."

BALANCING THE SCALES

Given that scales A and B balance perfectly, how many squares are needed to balance scale C?

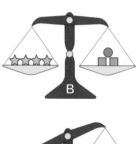

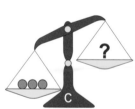

WHO AM I?

Bursting presence

I am:

_____

WHATEVER YOU DO, don't even THINK about...

Any of the following:

Your tax bill

Your credit card bill

Your gas bill

NAMED AND SHAMED

Clueless

_____

Fat butt

_____

Worst nasal hair

_____

PYRAMID PLUS

Every brick in this pyramid contains a number which is the sum of the two numbers below it, so that F=A+B, etc. No two bricks contain the same number, or just a zero, so work out the missing numbers!

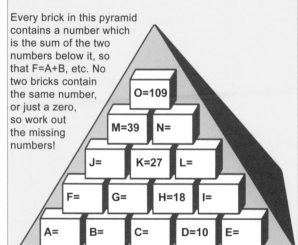

O=109

M=39   N=

J=   K=27   L=

F=   G=   H=18   I=

A=   B=   C=   D=10   E=

STARTING LINE

Which three-letter word can be placed at the start, to form three seven-letter words?

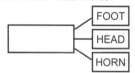

FOOT
HEAD
HORN

Answers to puzzles on the previous page

Whatever Next?:
2 – The letters move forward 2 letters, back 1, forward 3, back 1, forward 4, back 1, etc, so the next in sequence is O.
Couplings: 4/8, 6/5, 7/2, 10/11, 12/1, 13/3. The letters of 9 and 14 can be rearranged to form PARAGLIDING.

Jigsaw Crossword:

S	O	F	A		B		U	N	G
T		E	G	O		N		R	
O		R	E	F	U	G	E	E	
W	A	R		F		U	R	N	
A	M	E	R	I	C	A	N	A	
W	E	T		C		R	E	D	
A	N	I	S	E	E	D		I	
Y		N		R	Y	E		N	
S	I	G	H		E	D	G	E	

42

WEREWOLVES:

1 Offer tummy tickle

2 Give beef

3 Hide in shed

WAYS TO PASS THE TIME ...

Rowing ☐

Sewing ☐

Knitting scarves ☐

SUDOKU

The numbers from 1 to 9 inclusive need to be placed into the grid below in such a way that every horizontal row and vertical column contains nine different digits. In addition, each of the nine blocks of nine smaller squares should also contain nine different numbers. The clues are the numbers already placed.

	9				2		7	
2	3	7				6	8	9
		5		7	6	4		
		1	7				6	
3			4		9			8
	8				5	2		
		2	3	1		8		
9	4	8				3	1	6
	5		6				4	

WORDFILLER

Can you place all the listed words into the grid below?

3 letters
Mug
Tic

4 letters
Exit
Gala
Rust
Shun

5 letters
Atone
Brawn
Broom
Chute
Coral
Coypu
Hardy
Lyric
Nylon

Paste
Penny
Rayon
Salad
Tabby
Tense
Thorn
Tying
Yodel

7 letters
Eternal
Located

9 letters
Debutante

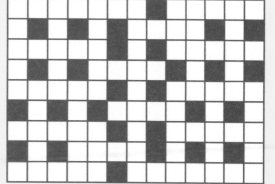

JOIN THE DOTS

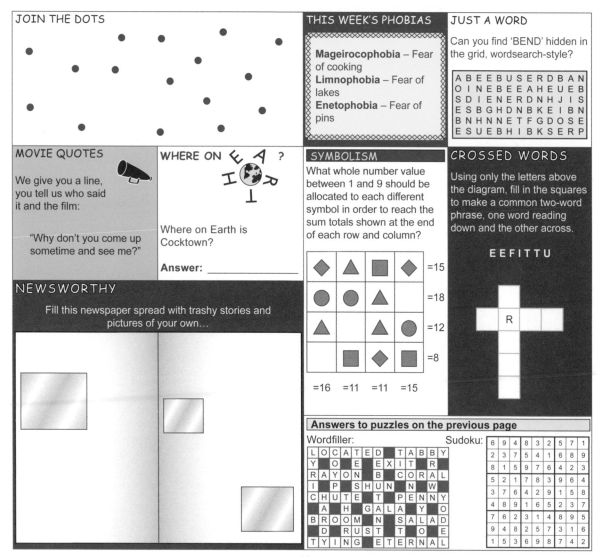

THIS WEEK'S PHOBIAS

Mageirocophobia – Fear of cooking
Limnophobia – Fear of lakes
Enetophobia – Fear of pins

JUST A WORD

Can you find 'BEND' hidden in the grid, wordsearch-style?

```
A B E E B U S E R D B A N
O I N E B E E A H E U E B
S D I E N E R D N H J I S
E S B G H D N B K E I B N
B N H N N E T F G D O S E
E S U E B H I B K S E R P
```

MOVIE QUOTES

We give you a line, you tell us who said it and the film:

"Why don't you come up sometime and see me?"

WHERE ON HEART?

Where on Earth is Cocktown?

Answer: _____

SYMBOLISM

What whole number value between 1 and 9 should be allocated to each different symbol in order to reach the sum totals shown at the end of each row and column?

◆ ▲ ■ ◆ =15
● ● ▲ =18
▲ ▲ ● =12
■ ◆ ■ =8

=16 =11 =11 =15

CROSSED WORDS

Using only the letters above the diagram, fill in the squares to make a common two-word phrase, one word reading down and the other across.

E E F I T T U

R

NEWSWORTHY

Fill this newspaper spread with trashy stories and pictures of your own...

Answers to puzzles on the previous page

Wordfiller:

```
L O C A T E D   T A B B Y
Y   O   E   E X I T   R
R A Y O N   B   C O R A L
I   P   S H U N   N   W
C H U T E   T   P E N N Y
  A   H   G A L A   Y   O
B R O O M   N   S A L A D
  D   R U S T   T   O   E
T Y I N G   E T E R N A L
```

Sudoku:

6	9	4	8	3	2	5	7	1
2	3	7	5	4	1	6	8	9
8	1	5	9	7	6	4	2	3
5	2	1	7	8	3	9	6	4
3	7	6	4	2	9	1	5	8
4	8	9	1	6	5	2	3	7
7	6	2	3	1	4	8	9	5
9	4	8	2	5	7	3	1	6
1	5	3	6	9	8	7	4	2

OUT OF PLACE

Two letters have already been placed in this grid; your job is to replace the remaining 18 to create four words reading across and five words reading down. To make things slightly easier, each letter must be placed in the row or column against which it appears; thus the first N must go in the first column and the first I must go in the top row. Good luck; beware of false starts!

```
        N   R   T   L   N
    I                       S
    E               D       U
    I                       A
    D       A               K
        C   A   S   E   E
```

BRAINTEASER

Which artist released both an album and movie entitled *Get Rich or Die Tryin'*?

TWO DOWN

Fit five of the seven listed words into the Across rows in the grid, so that the other two words read down the shaded columns numbered 2 and 3.

HATCH   NORSE
OCEAN   RELIC
SCALE   SLICE
      SNEER

```
1   2       3
4
5
6
7
```

NUMB-SKULL

Fit the listed numbers into the grid, crossword-fashion.

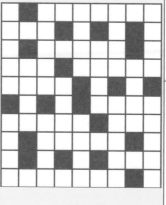

3 digits
303
327
439
542

4 digits
2011
2838
3031
3450
3738
5523
7342
7853
8254
8951
9005
9846

5 digits
13499
42775
45237
47531
51879
71530
78539
93949

7 digits
2437689
4187932

MUSIC TRIVIA

Who had a No 1 UK hit single in 1964 with *Little Red Rooster*?

Answers to puzzles on the previous page

Movie Quotes: Lady Lou (Mae West) *She Done Him Wrong* (1933)
Where on Earth?: Wexford, Ireland
Symbolism:
Circle = 8, Diamond = 6, Square = 1, Triangle = 2.
Crossed Words: Fruit tree

Just a Word:

```
A B E E B U S E R D B A N
O I N E B E E A H E U E B
S D I E N E R D N H J I S
E S B G H D N B K E I B N
B N H N N E T F G D O S E
E S U E B H I B K S E R P
```

BOX CLEVER

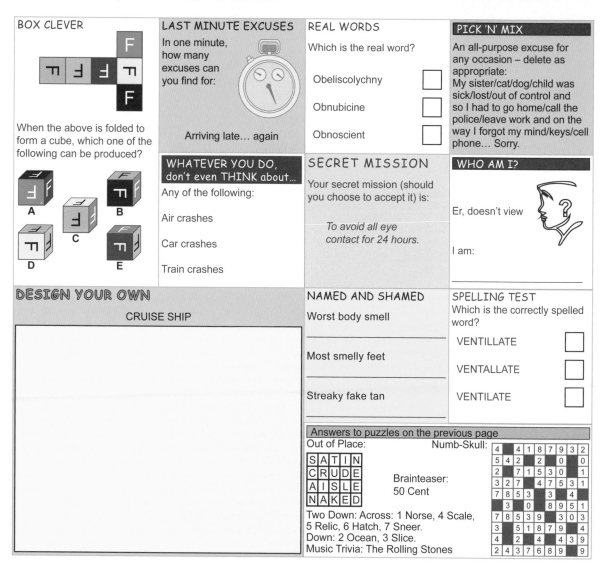

When the above is folded to form a cube, which one of the following can be produced?

A
B
C
D
E

LAST MINUTE EXCUSES

In one minute, how many excuses can you find for:

Arriving late... again

WHATEVER YOU DO, don't even THINK about...

Any of the following:

Air crashes

Car crashes

Train crashes

REAL WORDS

Which is the real word?

Obeliscolychny ☐

Obnubicine ☐

Obnoscient ☐

SECRET MISSION

Your secret mission (should you choose to accept it) is:

To avoid all eye contact for 24 hours.

PICK 'N' MIX

An all-purpose excuse for any occasion – delete as appropriate:
My sister/cat/dog/child was sick/lost/out of control and so I had to go home/call the police/leave work and on the way I forgot my mind/keys/cell phone... Sorry.

WHO AM I?

Er, doesn't view

I am:

_____

DESIGN YOUR OWN

CRUISE SHIP

NAMED AND SHAMED

Worst body smell

_____

Most smelly feet

_____

Streaky fake tan

_____

SPELLING TEST

Which is the correctly spelled word?

VENTILLATE ☐

VENTALLATE ☐

VENTILATE ☐

Answers to puzzles on the previous page

Out of Place:

S	A	T	I	N
C	R	U	D	E
A	I	S	L	E
N	A	K	E	D

Numb-Skull:

4		4	1	8	7	9	3	2
5	4	2		2		0		0
2		7	1	5	3	0		1
3	2	7		4	7	5	3	1
7	8	5	3		3		4	
	3		0		8	9	5	1
7	8	5	3	9		3	0	3
3		5	1	8	7	9		4
4		2		4		4	3	9
2	4	3	7	6	8	9		9

Brainteaser:
50 Cent

Two Down: Across: 1 Norse, 4 Scale, 5 Relic, 6 Hatch, 7 Sneer.
Down: 2 Ocean, 3 Slice.
Music Trivia: The Rolling Stones

KEYWORD

Simply fill in the letters missing from the different words numbered 1-6 and enter them into the numbered boxes, to reveal the hidden keyword. Take care, however, as some may have more than one possible letter which could fit: for example S — M E might be either SAME or SOME.

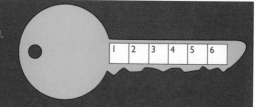

1	2	3	4	5	6

1 IN—ULAR
2 CHE—K
3 —ERVE
4 R—VEN
5 TU—OR
6 CL—AN

WORDSEARCH

Can you find all of the listed moons of the solar system in the grid? Words may run in either a forwards or backwards direction, horizontally, vertically or diagonally, but always in a straight, uninterrupted line.

AMALTHEA
ARIEL
ATLAS
CALLISTO
CALYPSO
DEIMOS
DIONE
EUROPA
GANYMEDE
IAPETUS
JANUS
LEDA
LUNA
MIMAS
OBERON
PANDORA
PHOBOS
PHOEBE
RHEA
TETHYS
TITAN
TRITON
UMBRIEL

```
N C R A E D E M Y N A G R
A O D R Z G S D R C P A H
L E R I N L I T X H W S E
L J G E A P I P S W L E A
V W A L B T Y A T L U N A
Z Q D N A O T K D M C O E
I M E N U L T P B A J I B
A A I U A S A R L W P D E
P L M S M N I L I H D W O
E P O A D E I T O T I H H
T U S O L S S B E U O M P
U H R E T T O C S T I N J
S A F O V S H R V M H A G
C A L Y P S O E A Y I Y I
V B Y R Z A F S A X Z L S
```

TOP FIVE

Best songs for a party:

1 _____

2 _____

3 _____

4 _____

5 _____

SWEET BAD MUSIC

So who on earth was responsible for this lyric?

"It's easier to leave than to be left behind
Leaving was never my proud"

SIMPLE AS A,B,C

In the grid, each row across, column down and diagonal line of six squares should contain two each of A, B and C. The clues relate to the squares only in that row or column. We give as many clues as we think you need (including any letters already in the grid), so can you place the letters correctly?

Across:
1 The Bs are next to each other.
2 No two squares containing the same letter are adjacent.
3 The As are further left than the Cs.
5 The A are between the Bs.
6 Each C is next to and right of a B.

Down:
1 The Cs are between the As.
2 The A are between the Bs.
3 The Cs are lower than the As.
5 One B is next to and below a C; the other is next to and above the other C.
6 Each A is next to and above a B.

WORD LADDER

Change one letter at a time (but not the position of any letter) to make a new word – and move from the word at the top of the ladder to the word at the bottom using the exact number of rungs provided.

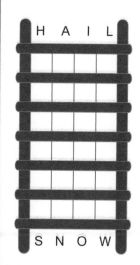

GOOD IMPRESSIONS

Can you pair up these door keys with the impressions of their ends?

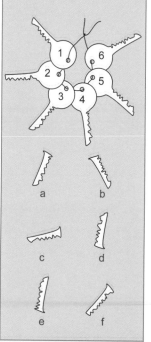

PRE-FAME NAME GAME

By what name do we know this famous person?

Susan Abigail Tomalin

ALL AT SEA

What was the name of Quint's fishing boat in the movie *Jaws*?

48

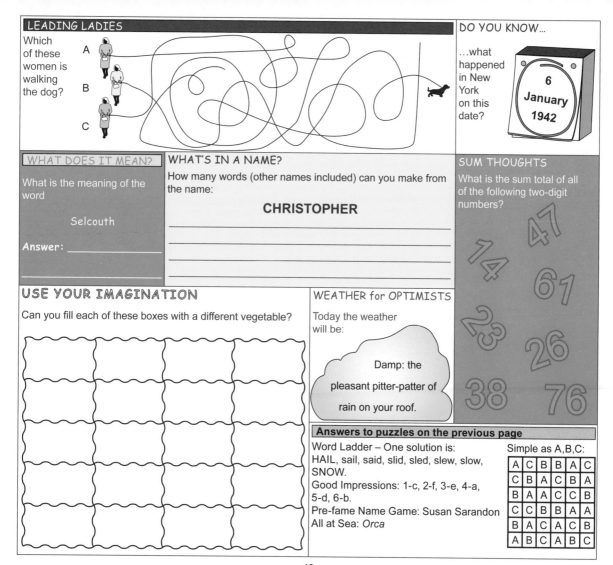

LEADING LADIES

Which of these women is walking the dog?

A

B

C

WHAT DOES IT MEAN?

What is the meaning of the word

Selcouth

Answer: _____

_____

WHAT'S IN A NAME?

How many words (other names included) can you make from the name:

CHRISTOPHER

_____

_____

_____

_____

SUM THOUGHTS

What is the sum total of all of the following two-digit numbers?

47

14

61

23

26

38

76

USE YOUR IMAGINATION

Can you fill each of these boxes with a different vegetable?

WEATHER for OPTIMISTS

Today the weather will be:

Damp: the pleasant pitter-patter of rain on your roof.

Answers to puzzles on the previous page

Word Ladder – One solution is:
HAIL, sail, said, slid, sled, slew, slow, SNOW.
Good Impressions: 1-c, 2-f, 3-e, 4-a, 5-d, 6-b.
Pre-fame Name Game: Susan Sarandon
All at Sea: *Orca*

Simple as A,B,C:

A	C	B	B	A	C
C	B	A	C	B	A
B	A	A	C	C	B
C	C	B	B	A	A
B	A	C	A	C	B
A	B	C	A	B	C

ON THE TILES

In this puzzle, the eight tiles on the right must be fitted into the pattern in the middle so as to form four words reading across and five words reading down. No tile may be rotated!

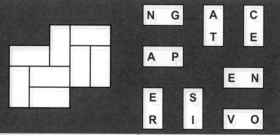

N | G
A
T
C
E
A | P
E | N
E
S
V | O
R
I

WEATHER for PESSIMISTS

Today the weather will be:

Bad enough to make you want to hibernate

AMAZING

Can you work your way from the entrance at the top to the exit at the bottom of this maze?

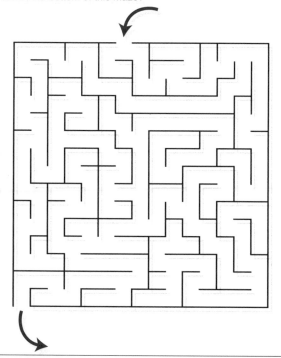

ROUNDWORD

Write the answer to each clue in a clockwise direction. Every solution overlaps the next by either one, two or three letters and each solution starts in its numbered section. The solution to the final clue ends with the letter in the first square.

1 Supply
2 Of the teeth
3 Count up
4 Dough raiser
5 Sports arena
6 Canadian province
7 Author of fables

Answers to puzzles on the previous page

Leading Ladies: Woman B
Do You Know…: A Pan American aircraft completed the first around-the-world commercial flight.
What Does It Mean?: Unfamiliar, rare, strange, wonderful.
Sum Thoughts: 285

WHO AM I?

Voice sells lot

I am:

_____

SECRET MISSION

Your secret mission (should you choose to accept it) is:

To speak as slowly as you can, making as little sense as possible.

STARTING LINE

Which three-letter word can be placed at the start, to form three seven-letter words?

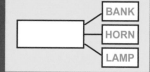

BANK

HORN

LAMP

MUSIC TRIVIA

Which group released the album *Regatta de Blanc* in 1979?

GET THE LOOK

Make the face:

CHILLED

IN CHAINS

This chain of letters contains the names of three types of building. The letters are in the correct order but need to be picked out.

TCEAFBMOPRLITEN

_____   _____

_____

CROSSWISE

Rearrange the six scrambled groups of letters to form words and then decide where each fits in the grid. Some letters are already in place.

AEGINU   AEHHRS
AEHLTW   AELNRV
DEEIMP   EIMMNU

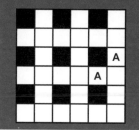

WHOLESOME FUN

In this puzzle, you need to find a five-letter word by deciding which common letter has been removed from the trios of words on each line.
Enter that letter into the circle at the end of each row and the word will be revealed reading downwards.

_AKE	PRO_	DO_N	◯
T_AT	_EAD	PIT_	◯
GA_N	TAX_	_CON	◯
_OAD	BOA_	IN_O	◯
P_EL	_DGE	FLO_	◯

LAST MINUTE EXCUSES

In one minute, how many excuses can you find for:

Not getting out of bed

Answers to puzzles on the previous page

On the Tiles:

Roundword: 1 Provide, 2 Dental, 3 Tally, 4 Yeast, 5 Stadium, 6 Manitoba, 7 Aesop.

Amazing:

51

TOP TEN

- RED
- GREEN
- PINK
- PURPLE
- ORANGE
- YELLOW
- TURQUOISE
- VIOLET
- WHITE
- CREAM

SPOT THE SAME

Only two of these modern abstract paintings are identical in every way: which?

THE NAME GAME

Can you complete the six words reading across in such a way as to reveal the name of a well-known person in the shaded columns?

	R	O		A
	A	P		D
	I	T		E
	O	L		Y
	N	D		R
	E	A		M

NUMBER BOX

In this puzzle, simply use the hints given to enter nine different numbers 1-9 in their correct boxes.

5 is next to and below 4
6 is further right than 8
7 is next to and above 9
2 is next to and right of 8
9 is next to and left of 4
7 is two squares above 3
1 is two squares below 2

ON TARGET

The answers to the clues read from the outer circle to the center, all ending with the same letter. When you've finished, the letters in the shaded ring will give a word.

1 Prod, usually with the elbow
2 Blockade
3 Item of dining room furniture
4 Exchange
5 Turning machine
6 Topic, motif

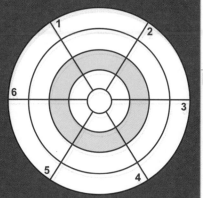

NIGHT ANIMALS

True or False:
Vampire bats feed on blood?

Answers to puzzles on the previous page

Who Am I?: Elvis Costello
Starting Line: FOG
Music Trivia: The Police
In Chains: Temple, Cabin and Fort.
Wholesome Fun: WHITE

Crosswise:

TOP FIVE

Best outfits for church:

1 _____
2 _____
3 _____
4 _____
5 _____

UNLIKELY CANDIDATE

FOOTBALL STAR

_____

CELEBRITY WRESTLING

HILLARY CLINTON

-V-

OPRAH WINFREY

UNFINISHED PICTURE

Can you complete this doodle?

DO YOU KNOW...

...what organization was founded on this date?

25 February 1919

JIGSAW CROSSWORD

Fit the blocks into the empty grid to form a complete crossword which, when finished, will be symmetrical, similar to the example seen here:

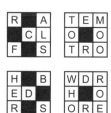

NAMED AND SHAMED

Slacker

_____

Having a nervous breakdown

_____

Last year's news

_____

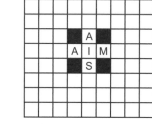

MOVIE QUOTES

We give you a line, you tell us who said it and the film:

"I'm going to make him an offer he can't refuse."

WHERE ON EARTH?

Where on Earth is Phuket?

Answer: _____

TODAY'S GREATEST ACHIEVEMENT

Clean underwear ☐

Being on time ☐

Landing a Boeing 747 ☐

IN SHAPE

How many triangles can you see here?

GET THE LOOK

Make the face:

EXCITED

DOMINOLOGICAL

What is the value of the question mark?

?

PYRAMID PLUS

Every brick in this pyramid contains a number which is the sum of the two numbers below it, so that F=A+B, etc. No two bricks contain the same number, or just a zero, so work out the missing numbers!

O=

M=43 N=

J= K= L=23

F= G= H= I=

A= B=9 C=3 D= E=18

WHO AM I?

O, fat male!

I am:

_____

Answers to puzzles on the previous page

Do You Know…:
The League of Nations

Jigsaw Crossword:

S	N	O	W	D	R	I	F	T
C		H		O			O	
A	R	B	O	R	E	T	U	M
R		A		A		H		B
	C	L	A	I	M	E	D	
F		S		S		R		S
A	B	A	T	E	M	E	N	T
N		O		O		O		U
G	A	S	T	R	O	P	O	D

54

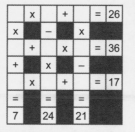

ELIMINATION

Every oval shape contains a different letter from A to K inclusive. Use the clues to determine their locations. Reference in the clues to 'due' means in any location along the same horizontal or vertical line.

1. A is due west of C and due north of I.

2. K is due south of G and due east of J.

3. H is due south of B, which is due west of D.

4. E is due north of J, which is due east of I.

5. F is due north of A.

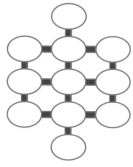

DESIGN YOUR OWN

ROOF GARDEN

MY NEXT PARTNER

Name:

_____

Occupation:

_____

Purchasing Power:

_____

TWO-WORD HOROSCOPES

Aries – shut up

Taurus – get out

Gemini – big surprise

Cancer – slow burner

Leo – bad luck

Virgo – strange experience

Libra – nice time

Scorpio – wrong way

Sagittarius – empty headed

Capricorn – why not?

Aquarius – pray… now!

Pisces – good times

Answers to puzzles on the previous page

What Does It Mean?: To be poisoned by cheese.
Brainteaser: Ronald Reagan
Letter Tracker: Puccini, Mussorgsky, Weber, Shostakovich, Stravinsky, Prokofiev, Mozart, Holst, Haydn, Schumann, Walton, Vivaldi, Wagner, Purcell, Handel, Verdi, Rossini.

Sum Total:

3	x	7	+	5
x		–		x
2	+	4	x	6
+		x		–
1	x	8	+	9

TOTAL CONCENTRATION

Can you fill in the missing numbers so that each row, each column and two longest diagonal lines meet the totals given?

							56
18	5		13		20	1	**70**
14		16	2	19	15		**87**
4	8			2	2	3	**49**
8	19	15		16	10		**80**
		6	4	9	12	18	**65**
1	20	9	17			8	**71**
7	7		12	3	19	8	**73**
63	**75**	**84**	**69**	**58**	**91**	**55**	**78**

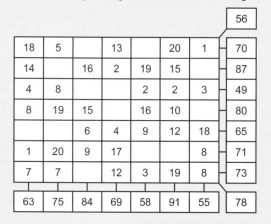

WORD LADDER

Change one letter at a time (but not the position of any letter) to make a new word – and move from the word at the top of the ladder to the word at the bottom using the exact number of rungs provided.

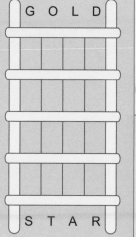

GOLD

STAR

STARTING LINE

Which three-letter word can be placed at the start, to form three seven-letter words?

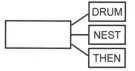

DRUM

NEST

THEN

WEATHER for OPTIMISTS

Today the weather will be:

Cold, with icy roads causing problems. A good day to stay off work.

TIED UP AT PRESENT

Which boy is holding the string attached to the present?

TWO DOWN

Fit five of the seven listed words into the Across rows in the grid, so that the other two words read down the shaded columns numbered 2 and 3.

ABATE   BRIDE
EDGED   HEADY
TIARA   TIRED
      TRAIN

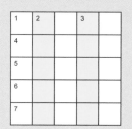

PICK 'N' MIX

Choose three words to describe your school:

Fun   Interesting
Enjoyable   Dull
Useless   Terrible
Painful   Busy
Girls   Boys

Answers to puzzles on the previous page

Elimination:

CLOCKWORDS

It's a race against the clock... How many common words of three or more different letters can you make from those on the clock face (without using plurals, proper nouns or abbreviations) in ten minutes? All words must contain BOTH the letters indicated by the hands on the clock.

QUOTE OF THE DAY

"My reputation grows with every failure."
George Bernard Shaw

WEATHER for PESSIMISTS

Today the weather will be:

Cold enough to cause frostbite

DICEY ARITHMETIC

Using three of the arithmetical signs ÷, −, x and +, can you achieve the correct total?

    =

BERMUDA TRIANGLE

Travel through the 'Bermuda Triangle' by visiting one room at a time and collecting a letter from each. You can enter the outside passageway as often as you like, but can only visit each room once. When you've completed your tour, the 15 letters spell out a word.

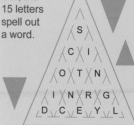

PROVERBS AND SAYINGS

The letters on the tiles were once all in place, but dropped out, falling in a straight line into the lower grid. Some tiles dropped earlier than others, so those on the lowest row aren't all from the same row in the grid above. Can you put them back into position in order to reveal a well-known proverb or saying?

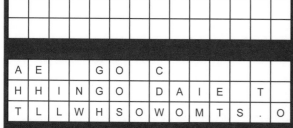

JOIN THE DOTS

Answers to puzzles on the previous page

Total Concentration: From left to right, top to bottom the missing numbers are: 7, 6, 11, 10, 14, 16, 5, 7, 11, 5, 3, 13 and 17.

Word Ladder – One solution is: GOLD, goad, road, roar, soar, STAR.

Starting Line: EAR

Tied up at Present: Boy B

Two Down: Across: 1 Abate, 4 Train, 5 Tiara, 6 Edged, 7 Heady. Down: 2 Bride, 3 Tired.

MISSING LINKS

Which word links the one on the left with the one on the right? We've done the first one, and when you've finished them all, the first letters of the link words will spell another word.

TALL	**STORY**	BOARD
CABLE		HORN
BLAST		PUTTING
MEAT		CHART
CAULIFLOWER		TRUMPET

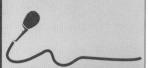
LETTER TRACKER

Begin in the central shaded square and follow a continuous path which will track from square to square, up, down and sideways, but never diagonally.

Your trail should cover every letter once only, in order to find:

Sixteen games, hobbies and pastimes.

V	I	D	I	M	A	G	I	R	G	N
I	O	K	E	R	Y	P	G	O	F	I
N	O	H	P	G	O	H	N	S	I	T
G	C	Y	A	R	T	O	I	H	I	T
Y	R	A	R	A	R	D	E	N	N	K
S	E	H	C	G	R	E	A	I	N	G
W	N	C	I	G	K	L	D	G	B	A
I	A	G	N	N	I	A	I	N	E	S
M	D	W	E	M	B	W	S	S	B	A
M	G	E	G	N	R	D	E	E	H	L
I	N	A	V	I	O	I	R	Y	C	L

SWEET BAD MUSIC

So who on earth was responsible for this lyric?

"I ain't never seen
An ass like that
The way you move it
You make my pee-pee go
'Doing-doing-doing'."

MISSING LETTERS

One letter of the alphabet is missing from each box. Find them all and place them in the order of the numbered boxes to reveal a six-letter word.

Word: _____

1	2	3
NGCXO	NHTBU	XYAQJ
WSMIF	VCOIM	RFBKW
RUZJA	PGWSD	LSCPG
DPYBK	JQXEL	HTZMD
HQELT	FRYZK	IOUEV

4	5	6
MWXAN	GPXAQ	UETIN
HLVBO	KBWJR	JVZBO
PUYCF	COZFL	CYSKF
GQKDT	MHUDV	GQDLP
JRZES	NEYIT	RXWAM

BOX CLEVER

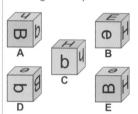

When the above is folded to form a cube, which one of the following can be produced?

A B C D E

WORDWHEEL

Using only the letters in the Wordwheel, you have ten minutes to find as many words as possible, none of which may be plurals, foreign words or proper nouns. Each word must be of three letters or more, all must contain the central letter and letters can only be used once in every word. There is at least one nine-letter word in the wheel.

Nine-letter word: _____

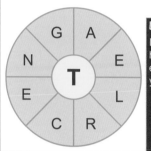

LAST MINUTE EXCUSES

In one minute, how many excuses can you find for:

Super-sized fast food

TOP TEN

SALMON ☐

TROUT ☐

SHARK ☐

OCTOPUS ☐

COD ☐

PLAICE ☐

SQUID ☐

HALIBUT ☐

SWORDFISH ☐

STURGEON ☐

CHARACTER ASSIGNATION

Fill in the answers to the clues, across the grid. Then read down the diagonal line of seven squares, to reveal:
The title of a play by Shakespeare.

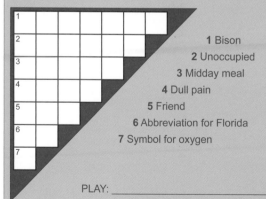

1 Bison
2 Unoccupied
3 Midday meal
4 Dull pain
5 Friend
6 Abbreviation for Florida
7 Symbol for oxygen

PLAY: _____

WHATEVER YOU DO, don't even THINK about...

Any of the following:

Your ex-boyfriend/ex-girlfriend

Your ex-boss

Your new boss

SPELLING TEST

Which is the correctly spelled word?

ACCOMMODATE ☐

ACOMMODATE ☐

ACCOMODATE ☐

Answers to puzzles on the previous page

Missing Links: Story, Car, Off, Pie, Ear. Thus: SCOPE
Music Trivia: Frankie Valli
Letter Tracker: Reading, Baseball, Chess, Walking, Gardening, Knitting, Fishing, Origami, Diving, Cookery, Photography, Archery, Swimming, Dancing, Weaving, Embroidery.
Sweet Bad Music: Eminem *Ass Like That*
Missing Letters: VANISH

BROKEN-HEARTED

Don't be halfhearted in your attempts to get these couples back together again! Match both sides of each heart, to reveal their names.

_____ & _____   _____ & _____   _____ & _____

_____ & _____   _____ & _____   _____ & _____

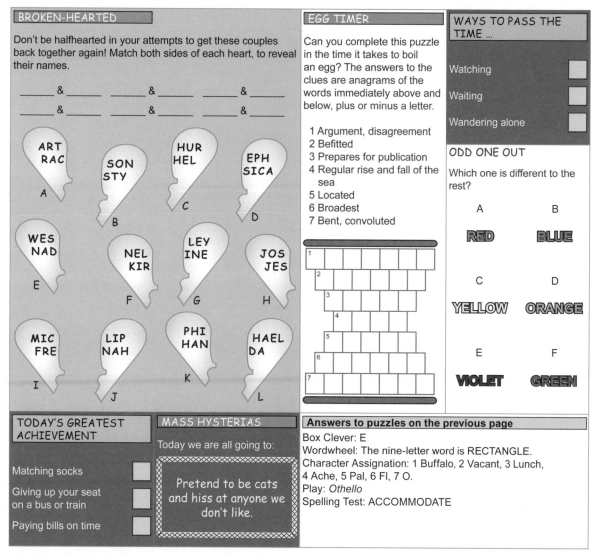

A — ART RAC

B — SON STY

C — HUR HEL

D — EPH SICA

E — WES NAD

F — NEL KIR

G — LEY INE

H — JOS JES

I — MIC FRE

J — LIP NAH

K — PHI HAN

L — HAEL DA

Answers to puzzles on the previous page

Box Clever: E
Wordwheel: The nine-letter word is RECTANGLE.
Character Assignation: 1 Buffalo, 2 Vacant, 3 Lunch, 4 Ache, 5 Pal, 6 Fl, 7 O.
Play: *Othello*
Spelling Test: ACCOMMODATE

ON THE TILES

In this puzzle, the eight tiles on the right must be fitted into the pattern in the middle so as to form four words reading across and five words reading down. No tile may be rotated!

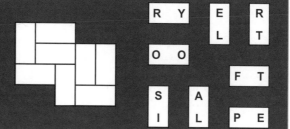

LOOSE VOWELS

Someone has taken all the vowels out of what was once a completed crossword. Can you put them all back in again? You should use only those letters beneath the grid.

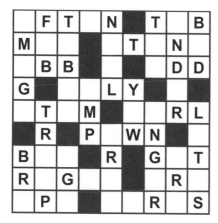

A A A A A A A A A
E E E E E E E E E E
I I
O O O O O O O
U U U U

A MATCHING PAIR

Which are the only two that are identical in every way?

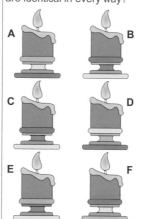

A   B

C   D

E   F

Answers to puzzles on the previous page

Broken-hearted: A and C, E and G, F and B, H and D, I and L, K and J.
Egg Timer: 1 Dispute, 2 Suited, 3 Edits, 4 Tide, 5 Sited, 6 Widest, 7 Twisted.
Odd One Out: E – It is not written in the colour it reads.

DESIGN YOUR OWN

SUPERMARKET

PAIR SHAPES

In the box below there are shapes in three different colors, red, white and blue. Any shape may have been rotated, but can you see which is the only shape to appear exactly twice in exactly the same color?

REAL WORDS

Which is the real word?

Bodillescious ☐

Boustrophedon ☐

Bognomania ☐

STARTER LETTER

Write down one each of the listed items, all of which must begin with the starter letter:

D

Country	
Tree	
Boy's name	
Girl's name	
River	
City	
Animal	
Make of car	
Drink	

CROSSED WORDS

Using only the letters above the diagram, fill in the squares to make a common two-word phrase, one word reading down and the other across.

A A C D H N S Y

PRE-FAME NAME GAME

By what name do we know this famous person?

Samuel Langhorne Clemens

MY NEXT PARTY

Place:
_____

Who's There:
_____

Occasion:
_____

Answers to puzzles on the previous page

On the Tiles:

A	F	T		
L	O	O	S	E
P	E	R	I	L
		T	R	Y

Loose Vowels:

O	F	T	E	N		T	U	B
M	O	A		A	T	O	N	E
E	B	B		I		O	D	D
G		O	I	L	Y		E	
A	T	O	M		E	A	R	L
	R		P	A	W	N		U
B	O	A		R		G	E	T
R	O	G	U	E		E	R	E
A	P	E		A	U	R	A	S

A Matching Pair: B and C

63

CODEWORD

This is a crossword puzzle in code. Every number represents a different letter of the alphabet and this number remains the same throughout the puzzle. Use the letters either side of the grid as well as the check-box below the grid to keep a track on your progress.

A B C D E F G H I J K L M

N O P Q R S T U V W X Y Z

A	26 **S**	2 **A**	1 **T**	26	22	19	2	■	13	2	4	10	2	26	26
B	17	■	18	■	11	■	7	5	2	■	■	5	■	12	■
C	2	21	2	4	10	■	21	■	12	2	11	1	8	5	20
D	19	■	20	■	5	16	18	7	5	■	■	4	■	4	■
E	12	26	2	7	19	■	11	■	■	■	1	8	5	18	20
F	■	9	■	■	12	20	6	23	23	5	20	■	■	5	■
G	9	22	18	7	1	■	■	■	7	■	2	19	2	26	26
H	■	5	■	15	■	4	8	2	18	11	■	3	■	4	
I/J	10	5	15	11	6	1	5	■	11	■	26	1	2	18	20
K	■	14	■	4	■	■	25	18	3	■	18	■	12	■	5
L/M	21	5	5	8	18	24	5	■	5	16	1	20	5	19	5

1	2	3	4	5	6	7	8	9	10	11	12	13
T	A											

14	15	16	17	18	19	20	21	22	23	24	25	26
												S

A IS TO B

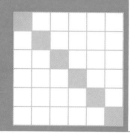

A is to *B*

as *C* is to

D   E

F   G

ARRANGING THINGS

If you fit six of these seven words into the grid, the word left over will appear reading down the shaded squares.

ABROAD   AGHAST
DAINTY   DIRECT
LICHEN   PAUNCH
SQUEAK

Answers to puzzles on the previous page

Pair Shapes:
Real Words: Boustrophedon
Crossed Words: Daisy chain
Pre-fame Name Game: Mark Twain

64

EYE-SPY

I spy with my little eye something beginning with:

_____

MIRROR WRITING

Write this word upside down:

BOLTING

_____

DO YOU KNOW...

...what was sent on this date?

16 August 1868

WHAT DOES IT MEAN?

What is the meaning of the word

Depone

Answer: _____

_____

COMPLETE THIS LIMERICK:

Whilst having a lovely hot bath

Young Harriet started to laugh

Her mum said "Dear daughter,

Don't do _that_ in water!"

_____

SWEET BAD MUSIC

So who on earth was responsible for this lyric?

"There were plants
And birds
And rocks
And things"

DOMINADDITION

Can you place the remaining dominoes in their correct positions, so that the total number of spots in each of the four rows and five columns equals the sum at the end of that row or column?

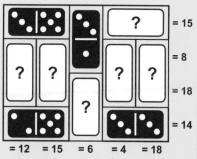

WHO AM I?

Hatchet mercenary

I am:

_____

Answers to puzzles on the previous page

A is to B:

G – The number of petals on the flower matches the number of leaves.

Arranging Things:
Across (from the top):
Dainty, Lichen, Abroad, Squeak, Paunch, Aghast.
Down: Direct.

Codeword:

S	A	T	S	U	M	A		J	A	C	K	A	S	S
W		I		N		L	E	A		E		P		
A	B	A	C	K		B		P	A	N	T	H	E	R
M		R		E	X	I	L	E			C		C	
P	S	A	L	M		N				T	H	E	I	R
	Q				P	R	O	F	F	E	R		E	
Q	U	I	L	T				L			A	M	A	S	S
	E		Y		C	H	A	I	N		G		C	
K	E	Y	N	O	T	E		N		S	T	A	I	R
	Z		C			D	I	G		I		P		E
B	E	E	H	I	V	E		E	X	T	R	E	M	E

Aries – lazy days

Taurus – hot pot

Gemini – bigger picture

Cancer – small gains

Leo – big news

Virgo – bad eyesight

Libra – grow up

Scorpio – miserable morning

Sagittarius – go home

Capricorn – happy days

Aquarius – don't think!

Pisces – go home

SHAPE RECOGNITION

Which are the only three pieces which will fit together to form a copy of this black shape?

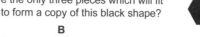

A B

C D

E F

H G

I J

WHO AM I?

Ten elite brains

I am:

_____

REAL WORDS

Which is the real word?

Carfax ☐

Calynorpious ☐

Caldivering ☐

SECRET MISSION

Your secret mission (should you choose to accept it) is:

To point out to your friends and family the essential pointlessness of their lives.

HEXAGONY

Can you place the hexagons in the grid, so that where any triangle touches another along a straight line, the contents of both are the same? One triangle is already filled.

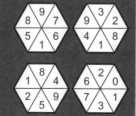

PRE-FAME NAME GAME

By what name do we know this famous person?

Harlean Carpentier

_____

MUSIC TRIVIA

Who had a hit in 1985 with *One More Night*?

Answers to puzzles on the previous page

Do You Know…: The first telegraph across the Atlantic.

What Does It Mean?: To testify under oath

Sweet Bad Music: America *Horse with No Name*

Who Am I?: Heather McCartney

Dominaddition:

3	5	3	0	4
1	1	1	0	5
6	4	1	1	6
2	5	1	3	3

66

SNAKES AND LADDERS

This is a standard game, so when you land at the foot of a ladder, you climb it; and when you land on the head of a snake, you slide down its tail. You need to throw an exact number to land on 100 to win – counting backwards if you don't, eg if you land on 98 and throw a five, you will end up on 97. The dice is thrown for you and always lands in this recurring order: 5, 3, 1, 2, 6, 4, so you can start by immediately placing your counter on square 5. Good luck – hope you win!

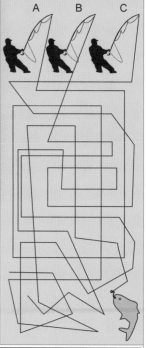

TANGLED TACKLE

Which of these anglers has landed the fish?

A   B   C

PATCHWORK

Fit the letters A, B, C, D, E and F into the grid below, so that every horizontal row, every vertical column and every shape of six smaller squares contain six different letters. Some are already in place.

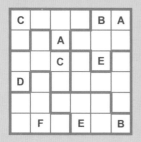

MOVIE QUOTES

We give you a line, you tell us who said it and the film:

"Carpe diem. Seize the day, boys. Make your lives extraordinary."

WHERE ON E A I R T ?

Where on Earth is Mount Mee?

Answer: _____

QUOTE OF THE DAY

"To succeed in the world it is not enough to be stupid, you must also be well-mannered."

Voltaire

Answers to puzzles on the previous page

Shape Recognition: B, E and H
Who Am I?: Albert Einstein
Real Words: Carfax
Pre-fame Name Game: Jean Harlow
Music Trivia: Phil Collins

Hexagony:

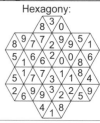

DICE-SECTION

Printed onto every one of the six numbered dice below are six letters (one per side), which can be rearranged to form the answer to each clue; however, some sides are invisible to you. Use the clues and write every answer into the grid. When correctly filled, the letters in the shaded squares, reading in the order 1 to 6, will spell out the name of an opera.

1 Bird of prey

2 Lazy person

3 Root vegetable

4 Blunder about

5 Begrudge

6 Disappear

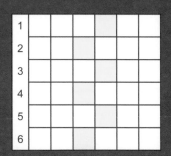

TOP TEN

SILK

NYLON

CASHMERE

VELVET

DENIM

COTTON

WOOL

ACRYLIC

CHIFFON

MUSLIN

ON TARGET

The answers to the clues read from the outer circle to the center, all ending with the same letter. When you've finished, the letters in the shaded ring will give a word.

1 Fox-faced primate

2 Guide, direct

3 Teacher

4 Mistake

5 Before

6 Obtain, receive

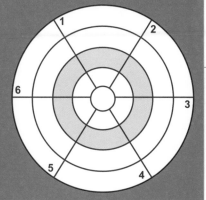

BRAINTEASER

What is the capital of the Caribbean island of Grenada?

Answers to puzzles on the previous page

Tangled Tackle: Angler A
Movie Quotes: John Keating (Robin Williams) *Dead Poets Society* (1989)
Where on Earth?: Queensland, Australia

Patchwork:

C	D	E	F	B	A
B	E	A	C	D	F
F	A	C	B	E	D
D	C	B	A	F	E
E	B	F	D	A	C
A	F	D	E	C	B

Which of the numbered alternatives comes next in this sequence:

| F | L | D | J | B | ? |

1 — H
2 — R

3 — N
4 — Q

COUPLINGS

Apart from two, every word listed below can be coupled with one of the others to make another word or phrase. Rearrange the letters of the two which can't be paired together to form one word, the name of a large animal.

1 PENT	2 SPOUT
3 WATER	4 NATIVE
5 SIGN	6 HEAL
7 TONGUE	8 STEAM
9 BOAT	10 DRESSING
11 OUTER	12 STAR
13 SALAD	14 SPACE

Answer: _____

WEATHER for PESSIMISTS

Today the weather will be:

Mild, with thunderstorms hinting at worse to come

GET THE LOOK

Make the face:

EMBARRASSED

PICK 'N' MIX

Delete as appropriate:
Last night was mad/scary/ridiculous. My best friend/sister/cleaner came round and we had a big feast/drinking session/argument because I had acquired/destroyed/created their worst nightmare/car/holiday.

UNLIKELY CANDIDATE

AWARD-WINNING AUTHOR

_____

JIGSAW CROSSWORD

Fit the blocks into the empty grid to form a complete crossword which, when finished, will be symmetrical, similar to the example seen here:

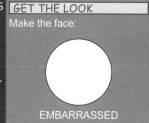

Answers to puzzles on the previous page

On Target: 1 Lemur, 2 Steer, 3 Tutor, 4 Error, 5 Prior, 6 Incur.
The word is: METRIC
Brainteaser: St George's

Dice-Section:

F	A	L	C	O	N
L	O	A	F	E	R
C	A	R	R	O	T
B	U	M	B	L	E
R	E	S	E	N	T
V	A	N	I	S	H

TODAY'S GREATEST ACHIEVEMENT

No hangover ☐

Salad for dinner ☐

Buying the first round of drinks ☐

MASS HYSTERIAS

Today we are all going to:

Go live in the mountains and worship snow.

THIS WEEK'S PHOBIAS

Symmetrophobia – Fear of symmetry
Theatrophobia – Fear of theaters
Geniophobia – Fear of chins

BALANCING THE SCALES

Given that scales A and B balance perfectly, how many squares are needed to balance scale C?

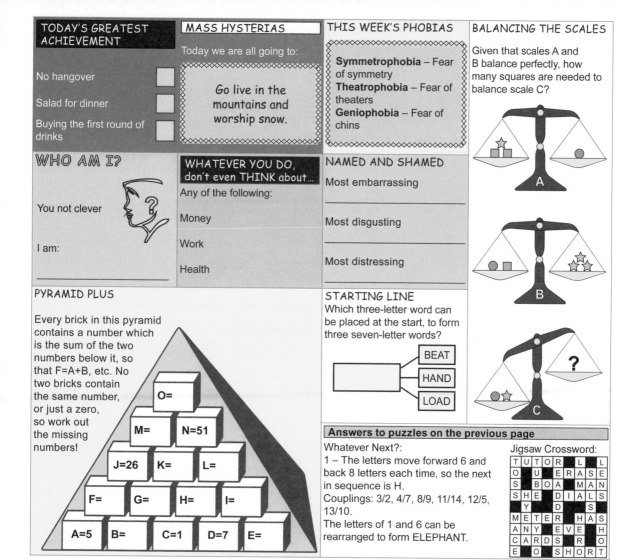

WHO AM I?

You not clever

I am:

_____

WHATEVER YOU DO, don't even THINK about...

Any of the following:

Money

Work

Health

NAMED AND SHAMED

Most embarrassing

_____

Most disgusting

_____

Most distressing

_____

PYRAMID PLUS

Every brick in this pyramid contains a number which is the sum of the two numbers below it, so that F=A+B, etc. No two bricks contain the same number, or just a zero, so work out the missing numbers!

O=

M=   N=51

J=26   K=   L=

F=   G=   H=   I=

A=5   B=   C=1   D=7   E=

STARTING LINE

Which three-letter word can be placed at the start, to form three seven-letter words?

[ ] — BEAT
[ ] — HAND
[ ] — LOAD

Answers to puzzles on the previous page

Whatever Next?:
1 – The letters move forward 6 and back 8 letters each time, so the next in sequence is H.
Couplings: 3/2, 4/7, 8/9, 11/14, 12/5, 13/10.
The letters of 1 and 6 can be rearranged to form ELEPHANT.

Jigsaw Crossword:

T	U	T	O	R		L		L
O		U		E	R	A	S	E
S		B	O	A		M	A	N
S	H	E		D	I	A	L	S
	Y		D			S		
M	E	T	E	R		H	A	S
A	N	Y		E	V	E		H
C	A	R	D	S		R		O
E		O		S	H	O	R	T

70

WAYS TO PASS THE TIME ...

Arguing ☐

Loving yourself ☐

Giggling ☐

WORDFILLER

Can you place all the listed words into the grid below?

3 letters	5 letters		7 letters
Doe	Acres	Miami	Satchel
His	Adieu	Puree	Slaving
	Aorta	Skill	
4 letters	Awash	Slant	9 letters
Aria	Claws	Steak	Groceries
Pole	Gamut	Taste	
Rain	Glass	Timid	
Tick	Hutch	Tripe	
	Irate	Until	

SUDOKU

The numbers from 1 to 9 inclusive need to be placed into the grid below in such a way that every horizontal row and vertical column contains nine different digits. In addition, each of the nine blocks of nine smaller squares should also contain nine different numbers. The clues are the numbers already placed.

6				9				4
	7	9	6		8	3	2	
		3	5		1	6		
9			1	6	4			7
	1	5				8	6	
7			8	5	9			1
		1	9		6	4		
	9	4	2		7	1	5	
3				1				2

JOIN THE DOTS

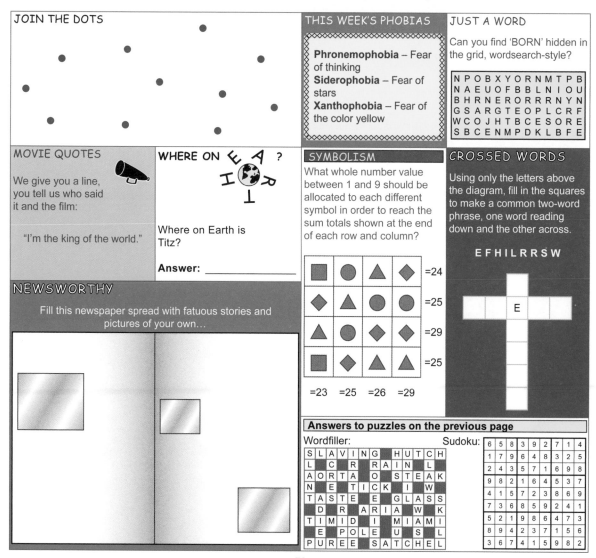

THIS WEEK'S PHOBIAS

Phronemophobia – Fear of thinking

Siderophobia – Fear of stars

Xanthophobia – Fear of the color yellow

JUST A WORD

Can you find 'BORN' hidden in the grid, wordsearch-style?

```
N P O B X Y O R N M T P B
N A E U O F B B L N I O U
B H R N E R O R R R N Y N
G S A R G T E O P L C R F
W C O J H T B C E S O R E
S B C E N M P D K L B F E
```

MOVIE QUOTES

We give you a line, you tell us who said it and the film:

"I'm the king of the world."

WHERE ON HEARТI ?

Where on Earth is Titz?

Answer: _____

NEWSWORTHY

Fill this newspaper spread with fatuous stories and pictures of your own…

SYMBOLISM

What whole number value between 1 and 9 should be allocated to each different symbol in order to reach the sum totals shown at the end of each row and column?

■	●	▲	◆	=24
◆	▲	●	●	=25
▲	●	◆	◆	=29
■	◆	▲	▲	=25
=23	=25	=26	=29	

CROSSED WORDS

Using only the letters above the diagram, fill in the squares to make a common two-word phrase, one word reading down and the other across.

E F H I L R R S W

E

Answers to puzzles on the previous page

Wordfiller:

```
S L A V I N G   H U T C H
L   C   R   R A I N   L
A O R T A   O   S T E A K
N   E   T I C K   I   W
T A S T E   E   G L A S S
  D   R   A R I A   W   K
T I M I D   I   M I A M I
  E   P O L E   U   S   L
P U R E E   S A T C H E L
```

Sudoku:

6	5	8	3	9	2	7	1	4
1	7	9	6	4	8	3	2	5
2	4	3	5	7	1	6	9	8
9	8	2	1	6	4	5	3	7
4	1	5	7	2	3	8	6	9
7	3	6	8	5	9	2	4	1
5	2	1	9	8	6	4	7	3
8	9	4	2	3	7	1	5	6
3	6	7	4	1	5	9	8	2

The answer to each of the following general knowledge questions is either 'a', 'b', 'c' or 'd'.

1 What was the first name of the 34th President of the USA?

  a. David   b. Daniel   c. Dwight   d. Duane

2 What is the capital of Barbados?

  a. Bridgetown   b. Port Louis   c. Barbados   d. Port Stanley

3 What is the surname of the author of *Wuthering Heights*?

  a. Binoche   b. Butler   c. Brontë   d. Benjamin

4 In which year was the Battle of Bunker Hill, in the American War of Independence?

  a. 1765   b. 1770   c. 1780   d. 1775

5 What was the first name of Mrs Thatcher, the UK's first female Prime Minister?

  a. Brenda   b. Margaret   c. Rosemary   d. Hilda

Which US rapper died when he was shot in a drive-by shooting on 13 September 1996 after watching Mike Tyson's comeback fight seven days earlier?

Fit five of the seven listed words into the Across rows in the grid, so that the other two words read down the shaded columns numbered 2 and 3.

CHEST   EDITS
MOCHA   MOPED
SMACK   SPEED
TERSE

Fit the listed numbers into the grid, crossword-fashion.

3 digits	5 digits
176	12110
299	24388
328	33757
364	49361
	59775
4 digits	65498
1675	73235
2577	91901
2845	
4901	**7 digits**
5886	2010285
5929	4114190
5965	
6191	
6824	
7539	
8941	
9134	

Who had a hit single in 1961 with *Runaway*?

Answers to puzzles on the previous page

Movie Quotes: Jack Dawson (Leonardo DiCaprio) *Titanic* (1997)
Where on Earth?: Germany
Symbolism:
Circle = 5, Diamond = 9,
Square = 4, Triangle = 6.
Crossed Words: Ferris wheel

Just a Word:

N	P	O	B	X	Y	O	R	N	M	T	P	B
N	A	E	U	O	F	B	B	L	**N**	I	O	U
B	H	R	N	E	R	O	R	**R**	R	N	Y	N
G	S	A	R	G	T	E	**O**	P	L	C	R	F
W	C	O	J	H	T	**B**	C	E	S	O	R	E
S	B	C	E	N	M	P	D	K	L	B	F	E

BOX CLEVER

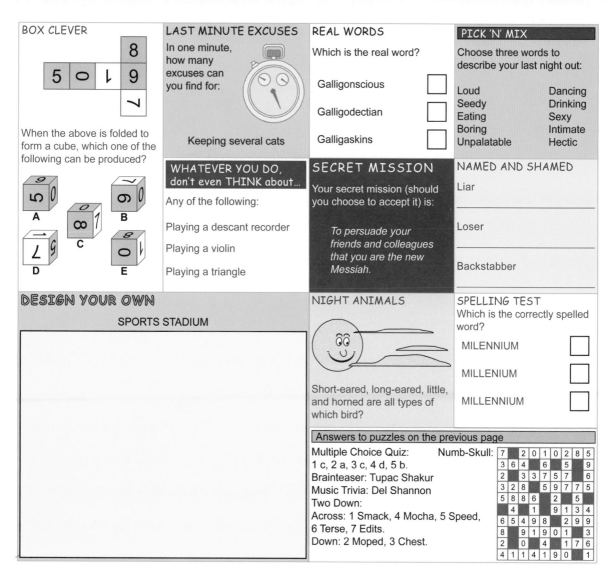

When the above is folded to form a cube, which one of the following can be produced?

A B C D E

LAST MINUTE EXCUSES

In one minute, how many excuses can you find for:

Keeping several cats

WHATEVER YOU DO, don't even THINK about...

Any of the following:

Playing a descant recorder

Playing a violin

Playing a triangle

REAL WORDS

Which is the real word?

Galligonscious ☐

Galligodectian ☐

Galligaskins ☐

SECRET MISSION

Your secret mission (should you choose to accept it) is:

To persuade your friends and colleagues that you are the new Messiah.

PICK 'N' MIX

Choose three words to describe your last night out:

Loud	Dancing
Seedy	Drinking
Eating	Sexy
Boring	Intimate
Unpalatable	Hectic

NAMED AND SHAMED

Liar

_____

Loser

_____

Backstabber

DESIGN YOUR OWN

SPORTS STADIUM

NIGHT ANIMALS

Short-eared, long-eared, little, and horned are all types of which bird?

SPELLING TEST

Which is the correctly spelled word?

MILENNIUM ☐

MILLENIUM ☐

MILLENNIUM ☐

Answers to puzzles on the previous page

Multiple Choice Quiz: Numb-Skull:
1 c, 2 a, 3 c, 4 d, 5 b.
Brainteaser: Tupac Shakur
Music Trivia: Del Shannon
Two Down:
Across: 1 Smack, 4 Mocha, 5 Speed,
6 Terse, 7 Edits.
Down: 2 Moped, 3 Chest.

KEYWORD

Simply fill in the letters missing from the different words numbered 1-6 and enter them into the numbered boxes, to reveal the hidden keyword. Take care, however, as some may have more than one possible letter which could fit: for example S — M E might be either SAME or SOME.

1	2	3	4	5	6

1 WH—LE
2 —RACE
3 ANT—ER
4 CATN—P
5 PRI—ED
6 KN—AD

WORDSEARCH

Can you find all of the listed coins in the grid? Words may run in either a forwards or backwards direction, horizontally, vertically or diagonally, but always in a straight, uninterrupted line.

ANGEL

BEZANT

COPPER

CROWN

DANDIPRAT

DIME

DUCAT

FLORIN

GROAT

GUILDER

GUINEA

```
T C S S T F W K P S J N G
O N O T D A N D I P R A T
K U A P A F J X C E E P N
V Q U Z P T P L A M L O I
E M I D E E E L Q Y A L D
V L A M N B R R N N H E C
O U B C X M M N G N T O R
T B E O D X E E O L Z N O
A G O F N P L L P Y G V W
O U V L C P D X E O E A N
R I Q O A O U I T K U E O
G L B R C E C R K B C N Y
F D G I X A A H E H L I D
V E T N O X T Q B B B T U N
C R I G N I L L I H S G L
```

NAPOLEON	PENNY	SIXPENCE
NICKEL	POUND	SOU
NOBLE	REAL	STATER
OBOL	SHILLING	THALER

TOP FIVE

Best songs for sunbathing:

1 _____

2 _____

3 _____

4 _____

5 _____

SWEET BAD MUSIC

So who on earth was responsible for this lyric?

"Time is like a clock in my heart"

SIMPLE AS A,B,C

In the grid, each row across, column down and diagonal line of six squares should contain two each of A, B and C. The clues relate to the squares only in that row or column. We give as many clues as we think you need (including any letters already in the grid), so can you place the letters correctly?

Across:
1 The As are between the Bs.
2 The As are not next to each other.
3 The As are further left than the Bs.
6 The As are further right than the Cs.

Down:
1 No A is next to and above a C.
2 The As are higher than the Bs.
4 The Bs are higher than the Cs.
5 The Cs are higher than the Bs.
6 The Cs are between the Bs.

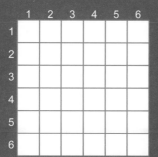

WORD LADDER

Change one letter at a time (but not the position of any letter) to make a new word – and move from the word at the top of the ladder to the word at the bottom using the exact number of rungs provided.

M O O N

B E A M

GOOD IMPRESSIONS

Can you pair up these door keys with the impressions of their ends?

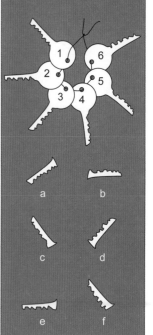

a

b

c

d

e

f

PRE-FAME NAME GAME

By what name do we know this famous person?

Virginia Wynette Pugh

ALL AT SEA

What was the name of the ship used by Squire Trelawney and Dr Livesey in the novel *Treasure Island*?

LEADING LADIES

Which of these women is walking the dog?

A

B

C

WHAT DOES IT MEAN?

What is the meaning of the word

Rastaquouere

Answer: _____

_____

WHAT'S IN A NAME?

How many words (other names included) can you make from the name:

GEORGINA

_____

_____

_____

_____

SUM THOUGHTS

What is the sum total of all of the following two-digit numbers?

29

40

31

77

12

55   62

USE YOUR IMAGINATION

Can you fill each of these boxes with a different breed of dog?

WEATHER for OPTIMISTS

Today the weather will be:

Wet, with heavy showers, so you can buy a nice new raincoat.

Answers to puzzles on the previous page

Word Ladder – One solution is:
MOON, boon, boor, boar, bear, BEAM
Good Impressions: 1-a, 2-e, 3-d, 4-c, 5-b, 6-f.
Pre-fame Name Game: Tammy Wynette
All at Sea: *Hispaniola*

Simple as A,B,C:

C	C	B	A	A	B
B	A	C	B	A	C
A	A	B	B	C	C
A	B	A	C	C	B
B	C	A	C	B	A
C	B	C	A	B	A

ON THE TILES

In this puzzle, the eight tiles on the right must be fitted into the pattern in the middle so as to form four words reading across and five words reading down. No tile may be rotated!

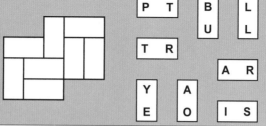

AMAZING

Can you work your way from the entrance at the top to the exit at the bottom of this maze?

ROUNDWORD

Write the answer to each clue in a clockwise direction. Every solution overlaps the next by either one, two or three letters and each solution starts in its numbered section. The solution to the final clue ends with the letter in the first square.

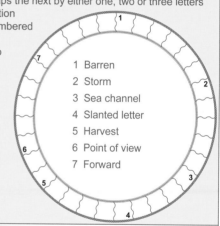

1 Barren
2 Storm
3 Sea channel
4 Slanted letter
5 Harvest
6 Point of view
7 Forward

Answers to puzzles on the previous page

Leading Ladies: Woman A
Do You Know…: The first rolled, perforated toilet paper.
What Does It Mean?: A social climber.
Sum Thoughts: 306

78

WHO AM I?

Pay Mr Clean Cut

I am:

_____

SECRET MISSION

Your secret mission (should you choose to accept it) is:

To roll your eyes every time anyone speaks to you.

STARTING LINE

Which three-letter word can be placed at the start, to form three seven-letter words?

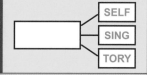

SELF

SING

TORY

MUSIC TRIVIA

Who had a hit in 1982 with *Maneater*?

GET THE LOOK

Make the face:

INEBRIATED

IN CHAINS

This chain of letters contains the names of three cities. The letters are in the correct order but need to be picked out.

ZMAOIGSRNLESBOK

_____   _____

_____

CROSSWISE

Rearrange the six scrambled groups of letters to form words and then decide where each fits in the grid. Some letters are already in place.

ACEGNY   ACHLNU
AELNRT   AENSUY
CCDELY   EINORS

WHOLESOME FUN

In this puzzle, you need to find a five-letter word by deciding which common letter has been removed from the trios of words on each line.
Enter that letter into the circle at the end of each row and the word will be revealed reading downwards.

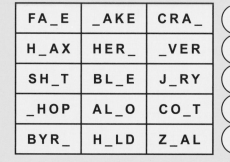

FA_E	_AKE	CRA_	◯
H_AX	HER_	_VER	◯
SH_T	BL_E	J_RY	◯
_HOP	AL_O	CO_T	◯
BYR_	H_LD	Z_AL	◯

LAST MINUTE EXCUSES

In one minute, how many excuses can you find for:

Speeding

TOP TEN

- BOOTS ☐
- SANDALS ☐
- STILETTOS ☐
- SLIPPERS ☐
- TRAINERS ☐
- BASEBALL BOOTS ☐
- BROGUES ☐
- BALLET SHOES ☐
- FLIP-FLOPS ☐
- BARE FEET ☐

SPOT THE SAME

Only two of these modern abstract paintings are identical in every way: which?

NUMBER BOX

In this puzzle, simply use the hints given to enter nine different numbers 1-9 in their correct boxes.

3 is next to and left of 8
5 is next to and right of 2
7 is two squares above 8
4 is further right than 9
2 is next to and below 1
6 is next to and left of 7

THE NAME GAME

Can you complete the six words reading across in such a way as to reveal the name of a well-known person in the shaded columns?

	H	A		E	
	W	A		T	
	O	A		T	
	I	G		T	
	N	L		T	
	N	T		Y	

NIGHT ANIMALS

What is the more common name for the bird sometimes called the goatsucker?

ON TARGET

The answers to the clues read from the outer circle to the center, all ending with the same letter. When you've finished, the letters in the shaded ring will give a word.

1 Find a solution
2 Animate, in existence
3 Appellation
4 Supple, lissome
5 Abnormally overweight
6 Poetry

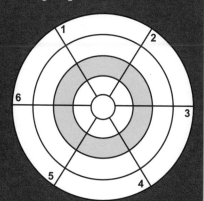

TOP FIVE

Best songs for being tearful:

1 _____
2 _____
3 _____
4 _____
5 _____

UNFINISHED PICTURE

Can you complete this doodle?

QUOTE OF THE DAY

"I seldom think of politics more than 18 hours a day."
Lyndon Johnson

UNLIKELY CANDIDATE

PRESIDENT

_____

DO YOU KNOW...

...which three-day battle ended on this date?

3 July 1863

JIGSAW CROSSWORD

Fit the blocks into the empty grid to form a complete crossword which, when finished, will be symmetrical, similar to the example seen here:

E	L	T
A		H
R	G	E

N	O	Y
	R	
T	E	A

F	E	E
	R	
A	I	T

R		B
A	S	O
P		W

A	N
S		D
C	H	

U	S	H
N		O
A	R	Y

N		B
	O	C	O
	D		U

R	E	A
M		M
S	T	E

C	L	A
A		C
L	E	N

	A	N
S		D
C	H	

NAMED AND SHAMED

Botox

_____

Detox

_____

Tummy tuck

_____

Answers to puzzles on the previous page

Spot the Same: A and D
The Name Game:
Chafe, Await, Roast, Right, Inlet, Entry.
Person: Carrie Fisher
On Target: 1 Solve, 2 Alive, 3 Title, 4 Lithe, 5 Obese, 6 Poetry.
The word is: LITTER
Night Animals: The nightjar

Number Box:

1	6	7
2	5	4
9	3	8

MOVIE QUOTES

We give you a line, you tell us who said it and the film:

"Of all the gin joints in all the towns in all the world, she walks into mine."

WHERE ON HEART?

Where on Earth is Ballville?

Answer: _____

TODAY'S GREATEST ACHIEVEMENT

Being a shoulder to cry on ☐

Eating no cookies ☐

Climbing a skyscraper ☐

IN SHAPE

How many rectangles can you see here?

GET THE LOOK

Make the face:

SICK

DOMINOLOGICAL

What is the value of the question mark?

PYRAMID PLUS

Every brick in this pyramid contains a number which is the sum of the two numbers below it, so that F=A+B, etc. No two bricks contain the same number, or just a zero, so work out the missing numbers!

O=

M=81 N=66

J= K= L=

F= G=25 H= I=5

A= B=9 C= D= E=

WHO AM I?

A saucier girl than I

I am:

_____

Answers to puzzles on the previous page

Do You Know…:
The Battle of Gettysburg

Jigsaw Crossword:

C	L	A	N		B	E	L	T
A		C	O	C	O	A		H
L	E	N	D		U	R	G	E
F	E	E		A	N	N	O	Y
	R		S		D		R	
A	I	T	C	H		T	E	A
R	E	A	R		B	U	S	H
M		M	A	S	O	N		O
S	T	E	P		W	A	R	Y

82

WHAT DOES IT MEAN?

What is the meaning of the word

Scopperloit

Answer: _____

_____

BRAINTEASER

Which country has the longest coastline?

WAYS TO PASS THE TIME ...

Dancing in public ☐

Busking ☐

Gossiping ☐

THIS WEEK'S PHOBIAS

Novercaphobia – Fear of your stepmother
Ideophobia – Fear of ideas
Kopophobia – Fear of fatigue

LETTER TRACKER

Begin in the central shaded square and follow a continuous path which will track from square to square, up, down and sideways, but never diagonally.

Your trail should cover every letter once only, in order to find:

Nineteen herbs.

P	E	P	S	R	A	P	Y	A	W	A
P	E	E	L	E	G	E	L	C	A	R
M	R	G	A	Y	A	V	O	Y	N	A
I	N	T	S	B	A	L	M	R	D	I
R	A	T	E	M	Y	H	T	A	E	R
R	A	I	L	S	M	A	R	M	R	O
O	G	V	V	A	C	E	J	E	R	C
N	E	R	O	R	Y	L	O	S	O	L
C	H	H	C	L	L	E	R	A	S	I
E	L	I	V	E	I	R	A	M	A	B
N	N	E	F	S	D	Y	N	I	S	E

SUM TOTAL

Place the digits 1-9, one per square, so that the sums are correct, according to the totals at the ends of the rows and columns. The calculations should be done in the order in which they appear, for example 6–2x5=20 should be read as 6–2(=4), then 4x5=20.

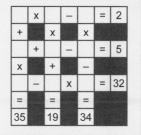

SECRET MISSION

Your secret mission (should you choose to accept it) is:

To come up with an idea for a best-selling book about donkeys.

BRIEF SURVIVAL GUIDE

SCHOOL:

1 Don't go

2 Plead insanity

3 Look interested

Answers to puzzles on the previous page

Movie Quotes: Rick Blaine (Humphrey Bogart) *Casablanca* (1942)
Where on Earth?: Ohio, USA
In Shape: 10.
Dominological: 1 at the top and 0 at the bottom; numbers decrease by one each time.
Pyramid Plus: A=4, B=9, C=16, D=2, E=3, F=13, G=25, H=18, I=5, J=38, K=43, L=23, M=81, N=66, O=147.
Who Am I?: Christina Aguilera

ELIMINATION

Every oval shape contains a different letter from A to K inclusive. Use the clues to determine their locations. Reference in the clues to 'due' means in any location along the same horizontal or vertical line.

1 A is due west of E and due north of G.

2 D is due west of B, which is due north of K.

3 C is due south of I, which is next to and due south of F.

4 J is due south of H, which is due east of D.

5 C is due west of K, which is further south than D.

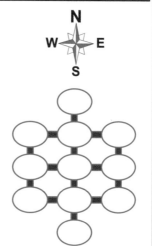

TWO-WORD HOROSCOPES

Aries – wait here

Taurus – lose it

Gemini – apple pie

Cancer – dare to

Leo – good riddance

Virgo – get busy

Libra – no more

Scorpio – useless day

Sagittarius – hey dude!

Capricorn – dark alleys

Aquarius – well now!

Pisces – try again

DESIGN YOUR OWN

HIDING PLACE

MY NEXT HOME

Place:
_____

Type:
_____

Price:
_____

Answers to puzzles on the previous page

What Does It Mean?: Rude or rough play.
Brainteaser: Canada
Letter Tracker: Marjoram, Anise, Basil, Coriander, Rosemary, Caraway, Lovage, Parsley, Balm, Thyme, Sage, Peppermint, Tarragon, Chervil, Savory, Celery, Dill, Chives, Fennel.

Sum Total:

4	x	2	–	6
+		x		x
3	+	9	–	7
x		+		–
5	–	1	x	8

TOTAL CONCENTRATION

Can you fill in the missing numbers so that each row, each column and two longest diagonal lines meet the totals given?

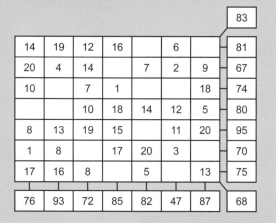

							83
14	19	12	16		6		81
20	4	14		7	2	9	67
10		7	1			18	74
		10	18	14	12	5	80
8	13	19	15		11	20	95
1	8		17	20	3		70
17	16	8		5		13	75
76	93	72	85	82	47	87	68

WORD LADDER

Change one letter at a time (but not the position of any letter) to make a new word – and move from the word at the top of the ladder to the word at the bottom using the exact number of rungs provided.

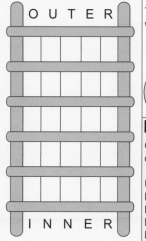

O U T E R

I N N E R

STARTING LINE

Which three-letter word can be placed at the start, to form three seven-letter words?

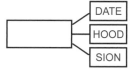

DATE
HOOD
SION

WEATHER for OPTIMISTS

Today the weather will be:

Cold with blizzards that will cause havoc, so you can relax by your fireside.

TIED UP AT PRESENT

Which boy is holding the string attached to the present?

TWO DOWN

Fit five of the seven listed words into the Across rows in the grid, so that the other two words read down the shaded columns numbered 2 and 3.

BASIN   GIANT
PLEAT   POINT
SALON   UNITY
USAGE

1	2		3	
4				
5				
6				
7				

PICK 'N' MIX

Choose three words to describe yourself when drunk:

Unconscious   Lost
Friendly   Excessive
Psychotic   Sexy
Drunken   Abstemious
Partying   Guzzling

Answers to puzzles on the previous page

Elimination:

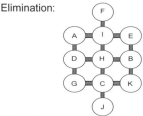

85

CLOCKWORDS

It's a race against the clock...
How many common words of three or more different letters can you make from those on the clock face (without using plurals, proper nouns or abbreviations) in ten minutes? All words must contain BOTH the letters indicated by the hands on the clock.

QUOTE OF THE DAY

"It was such a lovely day I thought it a pity to get up."

W Somerset Maugham

WEATHER for PESSIMISTS

Today the weather will be:

Quite spring-like, but it won't last

DICEY ARITHMETIC

Using three of the arithmetical signs ÷, −, x and +, can you achieve the correct total?

    =

BERMUDA TRIANGLE

Travel through the 'Bermuda Triangle' by visiting one room at a time and collecting a letter from each. You can enter the outside passageway as often as you like, but can only visit each room once. When you've completed your tour, the 15 letters spell out a word.

PROVERBS AND SAYINGS

The letters on the tiles were once all in place, but dropped out, falling in a straight line into the lower grid. Some tiles dropped earlier than others, so those on the lowest row aren't all from the same row in the grid above. Can you put them back into position in order to reveal a well-known proverb or saying?

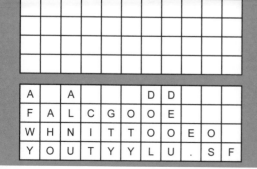

A		A				D	D		
F	A	L	C	G	O	O	E		
W	H	N	I	T	T	O	O	E	O
Y	O	U	T	Y	Y	L	U	.	S	F

JOIN THE DOTS

MISSING LINKS

Which word links the one on the left with the one on the right? We've done the first one, and when you've finished them all, the first letters of the link words will spell another word.

SEA	**SHORE**	LEAVE
CROSS		CHIMES
FLAT		CURTAIN
HIGH		TEACHER
BULK		GEAR

MUSIC TRIVIA

Who had a hit with *24 Hours from Tulsa* in 1963?

LETTER TRACKER

Begin in the central shaded square and follow a continuous path which will track from square to square, up, down and sideways, but never diagonally.

Your trail should cover every letter once only, in order to find:

Seventeen cities of the world.

L	A	N	T	A	N	N	A	H	J	K
T	A	G	B	S	E	L	J	O	A	Y
O	M	R	U	N	B	U	K	I	V	E
R	E	C	H	A	T	S	I	T	E	R
A	N	N	I	G	O	A	M	S	R	M
V	I	E	C	A	N	E	A	G	D	A
G	J	I	E	O	Y	W	I	O	T	A
N	I	O	B	R	K	S	T	B	O	M
A	I	R	A	L	L	A	N	O	G	O
C	E	R	S	M	A	O	D	L	W	S
L	A	T	N	O	D	N	N	O	O	C

SWEET BAD MUSIC

So who on earth was responsible for this lyric?

"I wish it was Sunday
That's my fun day
My I-don't-have-to-run day"

MISSING LETTERS

One letter of the alphabet is missing from each box. Find them all and place them in the order of the numbered boxes to reveal a six-letter word.

Word: _____

1	2	3
GRANX	UNEZF	OIDVM
BQMFW	MVDGT	PUCWH
CYPHO	HKWCS	XATFQ
DZILK	BPXIL	GBYNR
JTEUV	JQAYR	SEJZK

4	5	6
LAZRK	YIPVF	VGWAP
BYQHS	HOGWB	HBOIQ
MPJIT	NRCJZ	UEZCK
XCNFU	QDUXA	YDJMR
OGDVW	LSETK	TFXLS

Answers to puzzles on the previous page

Dicey Arithmetic: The signs are +, x and ÷.
Bermuda Triangle: INSTRUMENTATION
Proverbs and Sayings: A little of what you fancy does you good.

BOX CLEVER

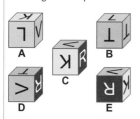

When the above is folded to form a cube, which one of the following can be produced?

A B C D E

WORDWHEEL

Using only the letters in the Wordwheel, you have ten minutes to find as many words as possible, none of which may be plurals, foreign words or proper nouns. Each word must be of three letters or more, all must contain the central letter and letters can only be used once in every word. There is at least one nine-letter word in the wheel.

Nine-letter word: _____

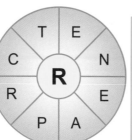

LAST MINUTE EXCUSES

In one minute, how many excuses can you find for:

Shopping

TOP TEN

CAR ☐

PLANE ☐

BOAT ☐

BICYCLE ☐

WALKING ☐

SCOOTER ☐

HORSEBACK ☐

TRUCK ☐

HOT-AIR BALLOON ☐

SLEIGH ☐

CHARACTER ASSIGNATION

Fill in the answers to the clues, across the grid. Then read down the diagonal line of seven squares, to reveal:
A character from Shakespeare's *The Tempest*.

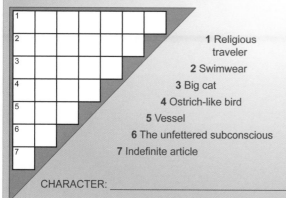

1 Religious traveler
2 Swimwear
3 Big cat
4 Ostrich-like bird
5 Vessel
6 The unfettered subconscious
7 Indefinite article

CHARACTER: _____

WHATEVER YOU DO, don't even THINK about...

Any of the following:

Your weight

Your love-life

Your hair

SPELLING TEST

Which is the correctly spelled word?

SERGANT ☐

SERGEANT ☐

SARGEANT ☐

Answers to puzzles on the previous page

Missing Links: Shore, Wind, Iron, School, Head. Thus: SWISH
Music Trivia: Gene Pitney
Letter Tracker: New York, Santiago, Bogata, Moscow, London, Dallas, Montreal, Cairo, Beijing, Vienna, Rome, Chicago, Amsterdam, Reykjavik, Istanbul, Johannesburg, Atlanta.
Sweet Bad Music: The Bangles *Manic Monday* (lyrics written by Prince)
Missing Letters: SOLEMN

Don't be halfhearted in your attempts to get these couples back together again! Match both sides of each heart, to reveal their names.

_____ & _____   _____ & _____   _____ & _____

_____ & _____   _____ & _____   _____ & _____

BOR GILL
A

YD ICA
B

TAIR BEL
C

IAN INE
D

ALIS ISA
E

JUL CEL
F

IS IAN
G

AMB LAU
H

BER OLI
I

TIE VIA
J

FLO MON
K

ROSE RA
L

EGG TIMER

Can you complete this puzzle in the time it takes to boil an egg? The answers to the clues are anagrams of the words immediately above and below, plus or minus a letter.

1 Last course of a meal
2 Directs, guides
3 Hair braid
4 Relaxation
5 Put away for later use
6 Hi-fi
7 Prize badge

WAYS TO PASS THE TIME …

Creeping

Laughing

Making toast

ODD ONE OUT

Which one is different to the rest?

A

B

C

D

E

F

TODAY'S GREATEST ACHIEVEMENT

Feeling serene

Feeling excited

Feeling forgiving

MASS HYSTERIAS

Today we are all going to:

Sell our houses and buy mobile homes.

Answers to puzzles on the previous page

Box Clever: E
Wordwheel: The nine-letter word is CARPENTER.
Character Assignation: 1 Pilgrim, 2 Bikini, 3 Tiger, 4 Rhea, 5 Urn, Tin or Can, 6 ID, 7 A.
Character: Miranda.
Spelling Test: SERGEANT

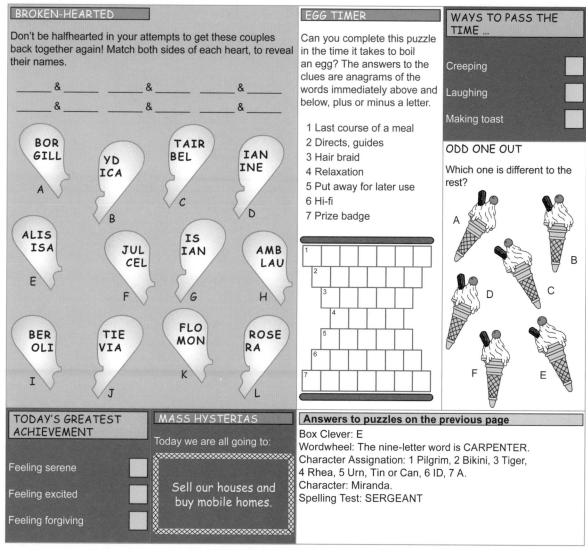

ON THE TILES

In this puzzle, the eight tiles on the right must be fitted into the pattern in the middle so as to form four words reading across and five words reading down. No tile may be rotated!

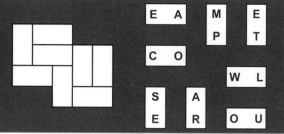

LOOSE VOWELS

Someone has taken all the vowels out of what was once a completed crossword. Can you put them all back in again? You should use only those letters beneath the grid.

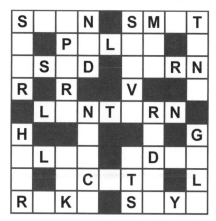

```
A A A A A A A A
E E E E E E E
I I I I
O O O O O O O O
U U U U
```

A MATCHING PAIR

Which are the only two that are identical in every way?

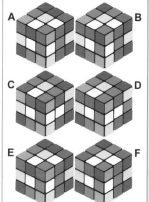

Answers to puzzles on the previous page

Broken-hearted: A and G, E and C, F and D, H and L, I and J, K and B.

Egg Timer: 1 Dessert, 2 Steers, 3 Tress, 4 Rest, 5 Store, 6 Stereo, 7 Rosette.

Odd One Out: E – The chocolate stick is shorter.

DESIGN YOUR OWN
APARTMENT BLOCK

PAIR SHAPES

In the box below there are shapes in three different colors, red, white and blue. Any shape may have been rotated, but can you see which is the only shape to appear exactly twice in exactly the same color?

REAL WORDS

Which is the real word?

Gongoozler ☐

Gongozeniar ☐

Gongenococity ☐

STARTER LETTER

Write down one each of the listed items, all of which must begin with the starter letter:

T

Country	
Tree	
Boy's name	
Girl's name	
River	
City	
Animal	
Make of car	
Drink	

CROSSED WORDS

Using only the letters above the diagram, fill in the squares to make a common two-word phrase, one word reading down and the other across.

A A E P P R S

| | O | | |

PRE-FAME NAME GAME

By what name do we know this famous person?

Jo Raquel Tejada

WHAT DOES IT MEAN?

What is the meaning of the word

Finnimbrun

Answer: _____

_____

Answers to puzzles on the previous page

On the Tiles:

A	W	L		
R	O	U	S	E
C	O	M	E	T
	P	E	A	

A Matching Pair: A and E

Loose Vowels:

S	O	O	N		S	M	U	T
O		P	O	L	I	O		U
U	S	E	D		E	A	R	N
R		R		V				A
	L	A	N	T	E	R	N	
H		I		O			O	G
A	L	O	E		I	D	E	A
I		A	C	U	T	E		L
R	A	K	E		S	O	Y	A

91

CODEWORD

This is a crossword puzzle in code. Every number represents a different letter of the alphabet and this number remains the same throughout the puzzle. Use the letters either side of the grid as well as the check-box below the grid to keep a track on your progress.

A B C D E F G H I J K L M (left side labels)

N O P Q R S T U V W X Y Z (right side labels)

13	17	9	18	24	16	24	■	6	20	25	23	16	4	6
24	■	6	■	16	■	18 T	24 I	N	■	■	16	■	9	■
13	23	14	23	22	■	17	■	5	23	22	18	26	24	16
24	■	23	■	18	24	3	6	22	■	■	24	■	11	■
14	1	9	4	24	■	■	■	■	22	6	24	11	6	
■	10	■	■	3	1	14	12	8	17	15	■	3	■	
9	6	10	6	3	■	■	■	17	■	17	9	13	16	5
■	9	■	10	■	■	22	7	23	17	18	■	24	■	9
17	22	14	6	18	24	14	■	16	■	19	6	16	16	17
■	6	■	16	■	■	17	21	18	■	6	■	24	■	16
25	6	9	18	23	9	26	■	2	17	22	19	13	17	12

| 1 | 2 | 3 | 4 | 5 | 6 | 7 | 8 | 9 | 10 | 11 | 12 | 13 |
| | | | | | | | | | | | | |

| 14 | 15 | 16 | 17 | 18 | 19 | 20 | 21 | 22 | 23 | 24 | 25 | 26 |
| | | N | | T | | | | | | I | | |

A IS TO B

A is to B

as C

is to

D   E

F   G

ARRANGING THINGS

If you fit six of these seven words into the grid, the word left over will appear reading down the shaded squares.

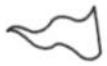

ASSIGN   HERESY
HIATUS   MAGGOT
METEOR   PAGODA
     PIGEON

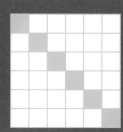

EYE-SPY

I spy with my little eye something beginning with:

_____

MIRROR WRITING

Write this word upside down:

POSTMAN

_____

DO YOU KNOW...

...what was signed on this date?

30 Sept 1938

PRE-FAME NAME GAME

By what name do we know this famous person?

Orison Whipple Hungerford, Jr

_____

COMPLETE THIS LIMERICK:

One day, at a quarter to three

Roseanne poured a nice cup of tea

Then she let down her hair

And relaxed in a chair

_____

SWEET BAD MUSIC

So who on earth was responsible for this lyric?

"I'm all out of faith
This is how I feel"

DOMINADDITION

Can you place the remaining dominoes in their correct positions, so that the total number of spots in each of the four rows and five columns equals the sum at the end of that row or column?

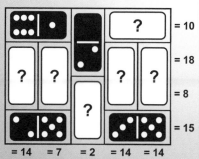

= 10
= 18
= 8
= 15

= 14   = 7   = 2   = 14   = 14

WHO AM I?

Will is Earthman

I am:

_____

WHO AM I?

On any screen

I am:

SHAPE RECOGNITION

Which are the only three pieces which will fit together to form a copy of this black shape?

A   B

C   D

E   F

H   G

I   J

SECRET MISSION

Your secret mission (should you choose to accept it) is:

To burrow deep down into the ground searching for a way to China.

SECRET MISSION

Your secret mission (should you choose to accept it) is:

To speak only in limericks all day.

REAL WORDS

Which is the real word?

Hornswobbit ☐

Haecceity ☐

Hornswiggle ☐

ALL AT SEA

In 1989, which ship hit a reef in Prince William Sound in Alaska, causing a major oil spill?

HEXAGONY

Can you place the hexagons in the grid, so that where any triangle touches another along a straight line, the contents of both are the same? One triangle is already filled.

PRE-FAME NAME GAME

By what name do we know this famous person?

Anna Maria Louisa Italiano

MUSIC TRIVIA

Who sang the TV theme tune to *Rawhide*?

Answers to puzzles on the previous page

Do You Know…:
The Munich Agreement.
Pre-fame Name Game: Ty Hardin
Sweet Bad Music: Natalie Imbruglia *Torn*
(lyrics written by Anne Preven)
Who Am I?: William Shatner

Dominaddition:

6	1	0	1	2
5	1	2	6	4
1	0	0	4	3
2	5	0	3	5

SNAKES AND LADDERS

This is a standard game, so when you land at the foot of a ladder, you climb it; and when you land on the head of a snake, you slide down its tail. You need to throw an exact number to land on 100 to win – counting backwards if you don't, eg if you land on 98 and throw a five, you will end up on 97. The dice is thrown for you and always lands in this recurring order: 2, 1, 6, 4, 3, 5, so you can start by immediately placing your counter on square 2. Good luck – hope you win!

100	99	98	97	96	95	94	93	92	91
81	82	83	84	85	86	87	88	89	90
80	79	78	77	76	75	74	73	72	71
61	62	63	64	65	66	67	68	69	70
60	59	58	57	56	55	54	53	52	51
41	42	43	44	45	46	47	48	49	50
40	39	38	37	36	35	34	33	32	31
21	22	23	24	25	26	27	28	29	30
20	19	18	17	16	15	14	13	12	11
1	2	3	4	5	6	7	8	9	10

TANGLED TACKLE

Which of these anglers has landed the fish?

A   B   C

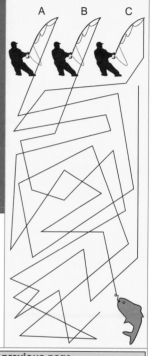

PATCHWORK

Fit the letters A, B, C, D, E and F into the grid below, so that every horizontal row, every vertical column and every shape of six smaller squares contain six different letters. Some are already in place.

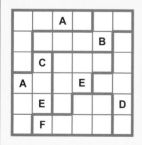

MOVIE QUOTES

We give you a line, you tell us who said it and the film:

"A census taker once tried to test me. I ate his liver with some fava beans and a nice Chianti."

QUOTE OF THE DAY

"I never think of the future: it comes soon enough."

Albert Einstein

WHERE ON EARTH?

Where on Earth is Lord Berkeley's Knob?

Answer: _____

DICE-SECTION

Printed onto every one of the six numbered dice below are six letters (one per side), which can be rearranged to form the answer to each clue; however, some sides are invisible to you. Use the clues and write every answer into the grid. When correctly filled, the letters in the shaded squares, reading in the order 1 to 6, will spell out the name of a capital city.

1   Small beetle

2   Very slim

3   Rule over

4   Straight

5   Fair-haired woman

6   Fervent partisan

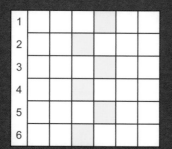

ON TARGET

The answers to the clues read from the outer circle to the center, all ending with the same letter. When you've finished, the letters in the shaded ring will give a word.

1   Additional payment or award

2   Shine

3   Infectious agent

4   S American mountain range

5   False name

6   Epicenter

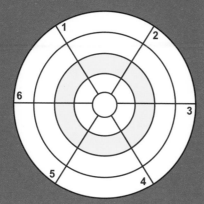

WEATHER for OPTIMISTS

Today the weather will be:

Wet at first, with worse rain later: think how good your garden's going to look!

TOP TEN

CAT

DOG

RABBIT

HAMSTER

MOUSE

PARROT

GUINEA PIG

HORSE

FISH

SNAKE

BRAINTEASER

Which country's national flag has the most colors?

Answers to puzzles on the previous page

Tangled Tackle: Angler C
Movie Quotes: Hannibal Lecter (Anthony Hopkins) *The Silence of the Lambs* (1991)
Where on Earth?: Sutherland, Scotland

Patchwork:

D	B	A	F	E	C
C	A	F	D	B	E
E	C	D	A	F	B
A	D	B	E	C	F
F	E	C	B	A	D
B	F	E	C	D	A

WHATEVER NEXT?

Which of the numbered alternatives comes next in this sequence:

| L | P | G | J | B | ? |

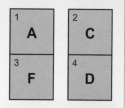

1 — A
2 — C
3 — F
4 — D

COUPLINGS

Apart from two, every word listed below can be coupled with one of the others to make another word or phrase. Rearrange the letters of the two which can't be paired together to form one word, the name of a famous alpine peak in Europe.

1 GLASS	2 BREAD
3 TWO	4 MOTH
5 ERRANT	6 CLAY
7 MOUTH	8 GOOD
9 LUCK	10 FACED
11 GINGER	12 RIVER
13 CHINA	14 CEILING

Answer: _____

WEATHER for PESSIMISTS

Today the weather will be:

Warm, with terrible levels of pollution

GET THE LOOK

Make the face:

WEARY

PICK 'N' MIX

Choose three words to describe your mother:

Domineering   Neurotic
Understanding   Daft
Considerate   Intelligent
Smothering   Critical
Egotistical   Kind

UNLIKELY CANDIDATE

WORLD LEADER

_____

JIGSAW CROSSWORD

Fit the blocks into the empty grid to form a complete crossword which, when finished, will be symmetrical, similar to the example seen here:

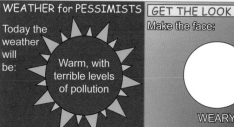

TODAY'S GREATEST ACHIEVEMENT

Phoning in sick ☐

Giving to charity ☐

Landscaping the garden ☐

MASS HYSTERIAS

Today we are all going to:

Paint our windows black so no one can see us.

THIS WEEK'S PHOBIAS

Gnomophobia – Fear of garden gnomes
Achluophobia – Fear of darkness
Venustraphobia – Fear of beautiful women

BALANCING THE SCALES

Given that scales A and B balance perfectly, how many circles are needed to balance scale C?

WHO AM I?

A churlish indoor minx

I am:

_____

WHATEVER YOU DO, don't even THINK about...

Any of the following:

Howling cats

Growling dogs

Biting ferrets

NAMED AND SHAMED

Bad breath
_____

Beer gut
_____

Flat feet

PYRAMID PLUS

Every brick in this pyramid contains a number which is the sum of the two numbers below it, so that F=A+B, etc. No two bricks contain the same number, or just a zero, so work out the missing numbers!

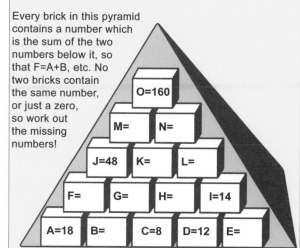

O=160

M=   N=

J=48   K=   L=

F=   G=   H=   I=14

A=18   B=   C=8   D=12   E=

STARTING LINE

Which three-letter word can be placed at the start, to form three seven-letter words?

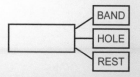

[___] — BAND
         HOLE
         REST

Answers to puzzles on the previous page

Whatever Next?:
4 – The letters move forward 4 letters, back 9, forward 3, back 8, etc, so the next in sequence is D.
Couplings: 1/14, 3/10, 8/9, 11/2, 12/7, 13/6.
The letters of 4 and 5 can be rearranged to form MATTERHORN.

Jigsaw Crossword:

H		S	T	I	R	R	U	P
E	R	A		L		H		A
R		T	I	L	D	E		G
E	V	E	R		R	A	G	E
	I		A	D	O		E	
T	E	A	T		O	M	E	N
A		T	E	M	P	O		O
I		O		A		O	U	R
L	I	M	I	T	E	D		M

WAYS TO PASS THE TIME ...

Writing ☐

Painting pictures ☐

Cleaning ☐

WORDFILLER

Can you place all the listed words into the grid below?

3 letters	5 letters	Money	7 letters
Bet	Aback	Ounce	Enclose
Key	Aware	Stoma	Yashmak
	Baste	Tawny	
4 letters	Bleak	Toner	9 letters
Cord	Brain	Trade	Everybody
Deed	Broom	White	
Oboe	Coati	Zebra	
View	Elbow	Zests	
	Hello		

SUDOKU

The numbers from 1 to 9 inclusive need to be placed into the grid below in such a way that every horizontal row and vertical column contains nine different digits. In addition, each of the nine blocks of nine smaller squares should also contain nine different numbers. The clues are the numbers already placed.

	3			7	8			5
			9			8	2	3
6		4			3	1		
		2		3			7	9
		5	7		1	2		
8	6			9		3		
		8	6			9		4
9	5	6			4			
7			2	1			8	

Answers to puzzles on the previous page

Balancing the Scales: 4
Who Am I?: Richard Milhous Nixon
Pyramid Plus: A=18, B=11, C=8, D=12, E=2, F=29, G=19, H=20, I=14, J=48, K=39, L=34, M=87, N=73, O=160.
Starting Line: ARM

IN CHAINS

This chain of letters contains the names of three cheeses. The letters are in the correct order but need to be picked out.

S G T E O I D L U T A D O M N A

_____   _____

_____

JUST A WORD

Can you find 'HARP' hidden in the grid, wordsearch-style?

```
H P R A C J A R P A H R T
N A E P P C H H A R P A H
D H R R T R E R T H M L P
H E R N C A R R S H E A P
F A H L R H S E A H T H V
H R T H R A E R E E A E R
```

MOVIE QUOTES

We give you a line, you tell us who said it and the film:

"No wire hangers, ever!"

WHERE ON  ?

Where on Earth is Lost?

Answer: _____

SYMBOLISM

What whole number value between 1 and 9 should be allocated to each different symbol in order to reach the sum totals shown at the end of each row and column?

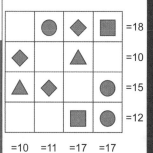

=10   =11   =17   =17

CROSSED WORDS

Using only the letters above the diagram, fill in the squares to make a common two-word phrase, one word reading down and the other across.

A D D E H N R T

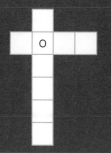

NEWSWORTHY

Fill this newspaper spread with highbrow stories and pictures of your own…

Answers to puzzles on the previous page

Wordfiller:

E	N	C	L	O	S	E		B	A	S	T	E
L		O		U		V	I	E	W		O	
B	R	A	I	N		E		T	A	W	N	Y
O		T		C	O	R	D		R		E	
W	H	I	T	E		Y		Z	E	B	R	A
	E		R		O	B	O	E		R		B
B	L	E	A	K		O		S	T	O	M	A
	L		D	E	E	D		T		O		C
M	O	N	E	Y		Y	A	S	H	M	A	K

Sudoku:

2	3	9	1	7	8	4	6	5
5	7	1	9	4	6	8	2	3
6	8	4	5	2	3	1	9	7
4	1	2	8	3	5	6	7	9
3	9	5	7	6	1	2	4	8
8	6	7	4	9	2	3	5	1
1	2	8	6	5	7	9	3	4
9	5	6	3	8	4	7	1	2
7	4	3	2	1	9	5	8	6

LETTER DROPS

The letters in the columns belong in the squares immediately beneath them, but not in the given order. Not all of the letters are used. When entered correctly, they reveal the names of four Hollywood stars.

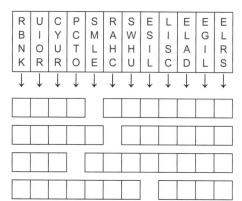

R	U	C	P	S	R	S	E	L	E	E	E
B	I	Y	C	M	A	W	S	I	L	G	L
N	O	U	T	L	H	H	I	S	A	I	R
K	R	R	O	E	C	U	L	C	D	L	S

↓ ↓ ↓ ↓ ↓ ↓ ↓ ↓ ↓ ↓ ↓ ↓

NUMB-SKULL

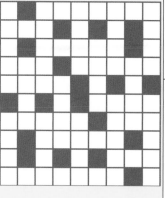

Fit the listed numbers into the grid, crossword-fashion.

3 digits
417
426
527
534

4 digits
1000
2003
2898
3815
4627
5063
7193
8802
8860
9009
9053
9163

5 digits
15741
30052
34060
37670
40219
55642
64996
85007

7 digits
3777818
7984351

MUSIC TRIVIA

Who had a hit single in 1974 with *The Streak*?

BRAINTEASER

Which actor, who died on 5 April 2008, was originally considered for the role of Chief Brody in the 1975 film *Jaws*?

TWO DOWN

Fit five of the seven listed words into the Across rows in the grid, so that the other two words read down the shaded columns numbered 2 and 3.

AZURE   COMIC
FLEET   RANGE
RIDGE   SNIDE
ZONAL

1	2		3	
4				
5				
6				
7				

Answers to puzzles on the previous page

In Chains: Stilton, Gouda and Edam.
Movie Quotes: Joan Crawford (Faye Dunaway) *Mommie Dearest* (1981)
Where on Earth?: The UK
Symbolism:
Circle = 5, Diamond = 6, Square = 7, Triangle = 4.
Crossed Words: Horned toad

Just a Word:

H	P	R	A	C	J	A	R	P	A	H	R	T
N	A	E	P	P	C	H	**H**	**A**	**R**	**P**	A	H
D	H	R	R	T	R	E	R	T	H	M	L	P
H	E	R	N	C	A	R	R	S	H	E	A	P
F	A	H	L	R	H	S	E	A	H	T	H	V
H	R	T	H	R	A	E	R	E	E	A	E	R

BOX CLEVER

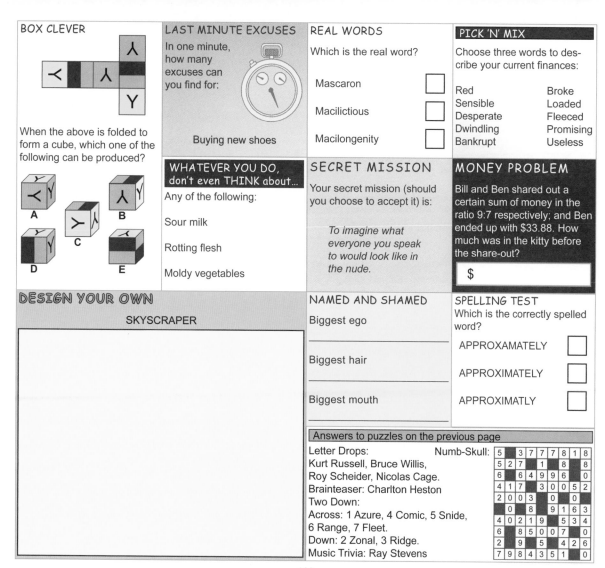

When the above is folded to form a cube, which one of the following can be produced?

A B C D E

LAST MINUTE EXCUSES

In one minute, how many excuses can you find for:

Buying new shoes

WHATEVER YOU DO, don't even THINK about...

Any of the following:

Sour milk

Rotting flesh

Moldy vegetables

REAL WORDS

Which is the real word?

Mascaron ☐

Macilictious ☐

Macilongenity ☐

SECRET MISSION

Your secret mission (should you choose to accept it) is:

To imagine what everyone you speak to would look like in the nude.

PICK 'N' MIX

Choose three words to describe your current finances:

Red   Broke
Sensible   Loaded
Desperate   Fleeced
Dwindling   Promising
Bankrupt   Useless

MONEY PROBLEM

Bill and Ben shared out a certain sum of money in the ratio 9:7 respectively; and Ben ended up with $33.88. How much was in the kitty before the share-out?

$ _____

DESIGN YOUR OWN

SKYSCRAPER

NAMED AND SHAMED

Biggest ego

_____

Biggest hair

_____

Biggest mouth

_____

SPELLING TEST

Which is the correctly spelled word?

APPROXAMATELY ☐

APPROXIMATELY ☐

APPROXIMATLY ☐

Answers to puzzles on the previous page

Letter Drops:
Kurt Russell, Bruce Willis,
Roy Scheider, Nicolas Cage.
Brainteaser: Charlton Heston
Two Down:
Across: 1 Azure, 4 Comic, 5 Snide,
6 Range, 7 Fleet.
Down: 2 Zonal, 3 Ridge.
Music Trivia: Ray Stevens

Numb-Skull:

5		3	7	7	7	8	1	8
5	2	7		1		8		8
6		6	4	9	9	6		0
4	1	7		3	0	0	5	2
2	0	0	3		0		0	
	0		8		9	1	6	3
4	0	2	1	9		5	3	4
6		8	5	0	0	7		0
2		9		5		4	2	6
7	9	8	4	3	5	1		0

KEYWORD

Simply fill in the letters missing from the different words numbered 1-6 and enter them into the numbered boxes, to reveal the hidden keyword. Take care, however, as some may have more than one possible letter which could fit: for example S — M E might be either SAME or SOME.

| 1 | 2 | 3 | 4 | 5 | 6 |

1 —EMAND
2 FAK—R
3 SPA—ED
4 T—KEN
5 H—NGER
6 RA—ID

WORDSEARCH

Can you find all of the listed words relating to children in the grid? Words may run in either a forwards or backwards direction, horizontally, vertically or diagonally, but always in a straight, uninterrupted line.

ADOLESCENT
BABY
BAMBINO
CHERUB
CHILD
HOYDEN
INFANT
JUVENILE
KID
LADDIE
LASSIE
MINOR
NIPPER
OFFSPRING
PUPIL

SCALLYWAG
SHAVER
STEPSON
STUDENT

TODDLER
URCHIN
WEAN
YOUNGSTER

```
W H D E L I N E V U J E I
N K I I W B I K R A T A H
A B K E M S A E S K J T I
N D A Y S T T M E M N C E
I N O A A S P O B E H I S
P H L L G D I T D I D H H
P T O N E N Z U L D N J A
E N U Y F S T D A K L O V
R O M A D S C L V F M E E
Y T N W G E Y E I I Y N R
S T E P S O N D N B N I T
C H E R U B B O A T Z H O
T T L G X P R B X Z E C C
O F F S P R I N G T E R Q
W L G A W Y L L A C S U U
```

TOP FIVE

Best songs for getting up:

1

2

3

4

5

SWEET BAD MUSIC

So who on earth was responsible for this lyric?

"Now you're amazed
By the VIP posse
Steppin' so hard
Like a German Nazi"

Answers to puzzles on the previous page

Box Clever: B
Real Words: Mascaron
Money Problem: There was $77.44 in the kitty and Ben got seven-sixteenths of this. Ben got $33.88 and Bill got $43.56.
Spelling Test: APPROXIMATELY

SIMPLE AS A,B,C

In the grid, each row across, column down and diagonal line of six squares should contain two each of A, B and C. The clues relate to the squares only in that row or column. We give as many clues as we think you need (including any letters already in the grid), so can you place the letters correctly?

Across:
1 The As are between the Cs.
3 The Cs are not next to each other.
4 The As are next to each other.
5 The As are further right than the Cs.
6 The As are further left than the Cs.

Down:
1 The Bs are between the As.
3 The Bs are between the As.
5 The Bs are between the As.
6 The As are lower than the Cs.

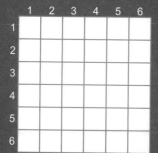

WORD LADDER

Change one letter at a time (but not the position of any letter) to make a new word – and move from the word at the top of the ladder to the word at the bottom using the exact number of rungs provided.

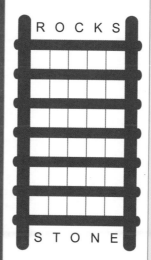

R O C K S

S T O N E

GOOD IMPRESSIONS

Can you pair up these door keys with the impressions of their ends?

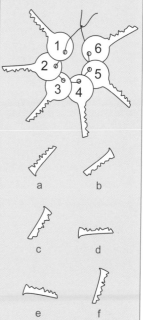

a

b

c

d

e

f

PRE-FAME NAME GAME

By what name do we know this famous person?

Margarita Cansino

ALL AT SEA

What is the name of the ferry service that links Hong Kong Island to Kowloon across Victoria Harbour?

104

LEADING LADIES

Which of these women is walking the dog?

A

B

C

DO YOU KNOW...

...what happened on this date?

14 October 1066

WHAT DOES IT MEAN?

What is the meaning of the word

Pronk

Answer: _____

_____

WHAT'S IN A NAME?

How many words (other names included) can you make from the name:

FRANCESCA

_____

_____

_____

_____

SUM THOUGHTS

What is the sum total of all of the following two-digit numbers?

49

42

16

25

19

64

50

USE YOUR IMAGINATION

Can you fill each of these boxes with a different movie title?

WEATHER for OPTIMISTS

Today the weather will be:

Rainy; the torrential rain will clean your car very nicely!

Answers to puzzles on the previous page

Word Ladder – One solution is: ROCKS, socks, soaks, soars, stars, stare, store, STONE.

Good Impressions: 1-f, 2-d, 3-a, 4-b, 5-e, 6-c.

Pre-fame Name Game: Rita Hayworth

All at Sea: Star Ferry

Simple as A,B,C:

C	B	A	B	A	C
A	C	B	A	B	C
C	A	B	C	B	A
B	C	A	A	C	B
B	B	C	C	A	A
A	A	C	B	C	B

ON THE TILES

In this puzzle, the eight tiles on the right must be fitted into the pattern in the middle so as to form four words reading across and five words reading down. No tile may be rotated!

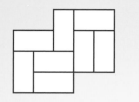

D	O		E		O	W
E	D				P	I
A		R				
R		R	E		C	A

AMAZING

Can you work your way from the entrance at the top to the exit at the bottom of this maze?

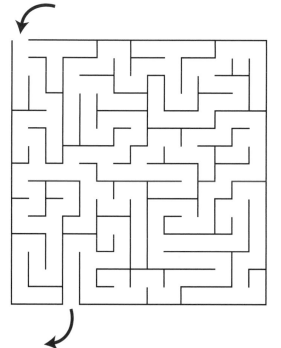

ROUNDWORD

Write the answer to each clue in a clockwise direction. Every solution overlaps the next by either one, two or three letters and each solution starts in its numbered section.

The solution to the final clue ends with the letter in the first square.

1 Break loose
2 Large-billed bird
3 Ship's brake
4 Public speaker
5 Coarse
6 Poor district of a city
7 Endure, put up with

Answers to puzzles on the previous page

Leading Ladies: Woman B
Do You Know…: The Battle of Hastings took place.
What Does It Mean?: A weak or foolish person OR to strut, prance or leap up.
Sum Thoughts: 265

JOIN THE DOTS

STARTING LINE

Which three-letter word can be placed at the start, to form three seven-letter words?

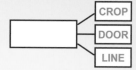

CROP

DOOR

LINE

MUSIC TRIVIA

Which Man in Black was also a Boy Named Sue?

GET THE LOOK

Make the face:

SELF-SATISFIED

IN CHAINS

This chain of letters contains the names of three vehicles. The letters are in the correct order but need to be picked out.

TSRCLAEODIAGCENH

_____   _____

_____

CROSSWISE

Rearrange the six scrambled groups of letters to form words and then decide where each fits in the grid. Some letters are already in place.

AEENNX	AEGLMN
AEGOVY	CLMNOU
EEELSS	FGNSUU

WHOLESOME FUN

In this puzzle, you need to find a five-letter word by deciding which common letter has been removed from the trios of words on each line.

Enter that letter into the circle at the end of each row and the word will be revealed reading downwards.

CO_L	_ISE	S_AB	◯
RAS_	W_AT	_OME	◯
B_RN	_IRY	CY_N	◯
PE_T	COA_	CO_T	◯
F_AR	FIR_	B_AK	◯

LAST MINUTE EXCUSES

In one minute, how many excuses can you find for:

A wild night out

107

TOP TEN

- APPLES ☐
- ORANGES ☐
- BANANAS ☐
- PINEAPPLES ☐
- PEARS ☐
- STRAWBERRIES ☐
- BLUEBERRIES ☐
- RASPBERRIES ☐
- PLUMS ☐
- CHERRIES ☐

SPOT THE SAME

Only two of these modern abstract paintings are identical in every way: which?

NUMBER BOX

In this puzzle, simply use the hints given to enter nine different numbers 1-9 in their correct boxes.

1 is two squares left of 6
3 is two squares above 4
7 is next to and right of 3
2 is between 6 and 7
8 is next to and right of 5

THE NAME GAME

Can you complete the six words reading across in such a way as to reveal the name of a well-known person in the shaded columns?

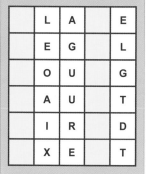

L	A		E
E	G		L
O	U		G
A	U		T
I	R		D
X	E		T

NIGHT ANIMALS

In a famous song of 1940, what type of bird sang in Berkeley Square?

ON TARGET

The answers to the clues read from the outer circle to the center, all ending with the same letter. When you've finished, the letters in the shaded ring will give a word.

1 Tall structure
2 Purring sound
3 Relating to the Sun
4 Layabout
5 Powdered cereal
6 Grass-cutter

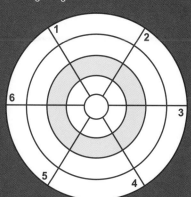

Answers to puzzles on the previous page

Starting Line: OUT
Music Trivia: Johnny Cash
In Chains: Train, Sledge and Coach.
Wholesome Fun: WHALE

Crosswise:

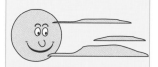

108

TOP FIVE

Best songs for leaving your lover:

1 _____
2 _____
3 _____
4 _____
5 _____

CELEBRITY WRESTLING

SHREK

-v-

DONALD DUCK

UNFINISHED PICTURE

Can you complete this doodle?

QUOTE OF THE DAY

"Fashion is a form of ugliness so intolerable that we have to alter it every six months."
Oscar Wilde

UNLIKELY CANDIDATE

BEST DRESSED FEMALE

_____

DO YOU KNOW...

...what happened in Buffalo, New York on this date?

6 Sept 1901

JIGSAW CROSSWORD

Fit the blocks into the empty grid to form a complete crossword which, when finished, will be symmetrical, similar to the example seen here:

NAMED AND SHAMED

Meanest

_____

Dreariest

_____

Weirdest

_____

MOVIE QUOTES

We give you a line, you tell us who said it and the film:

"Love means never having to say you're sorry."

WHERE ON EARTH?

Where on Earth is Little Dix?

Answer: _____

TODAY'S GREATEST ACHIEVEMENT

Not spending any money ☐

Cleaning the toilet ☐

Washing machine didn't flood ☐

IN SHAPE

How many circles can you see here?

GET THE LOOK

Make the face:

JEALOUS

DOMINOLOGICAL

What is the value of the question mark?

?

PYRAMID PLUS

Every brick in this pyramid contains a number which is the sum of the two numbers below it, so that F=A+B, etc. No two bricks contain the same number, or just a zero, so work out the missing numbers!

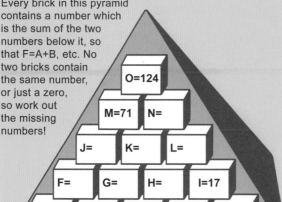

O=124

M=71 N=

J= K= L=

F= G= H= I=17

A= B=15 C=5 D= E=

WHO AM I?

Grunted minor songs

I am (name and nickname):

_____

Answers to puzzles on the previous page

Do You Know...:
President McKinley was assassinated.

Jigsaw Crossword:

R		S	Q	U	A	L	I	D
E	R	A		S		U		I
F		S	M	E	A	R		S
E	C	H	O		L	E	G	S
R		S	K	I				O
R	O	S	E		B	A	L	L
I		A	S	P	I	C		U
N		V		E		H	I	T
G	R	E	N	A	D	E		E

110

WHAT DOES IT MEAN?

What is the meaning of the word

Pulveratricious

Answer: _____

_____

BRAINTEASER

What is the name of the dam on the Zambia/Zimbabwe border?

WAYS TO PASS THE TIME …

Bathing ☐

Burning buildings ☐

Baking ☐

THIS WEEK'S PHOBIAS

Symbolophobia – Fear of symbolism
Papyrophobia – Fear of paper
Genuphobia – Fear of knees

LETTER TRACKER

Begin in the central shaded square and follow a continuous path which will track from square to square, up, down and sideways, but never diagonally.

Your trail should cover every letter once only, in order to find:

Sixteen islands.

E	I	C	E	L	A	N	R	I	T	Z
T	Y	L	I	C	I	D	T	N	I	B
E	R	I	C	A	S	I	L	I	P	E
U	C	A	M	A	J	A	A	D	S	R
H	O	H	E	U	S	T	R	A	D	G
S	N	I	F	A	G	R	E	E	N	E
B	A	R	E	D	N	A	L	N	S	A
U	T	E	N	M	U	S	R	R	A	R
C	L	I	T	A	S	C	A	B	B	D
A	A	R	R	G	A	M	S	A	A	I
K	N	S	A	A	D	A	O	D	I	N

SUM TOTAL

Place the digits 1-9, one per square, so that the sums are correct, according to the totals at the ends of the rows and columns. The calculations should be done in the order in which they appear, for example 6–2x5=20 should be read as 6–2(=4), then 4x5=20.

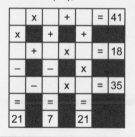

SECRET MISSION

Your secret mission (should you choose to accept it) is:

To set out on the road to Shangri-La, with only a toothbrush in your bag.

BRIEF SURVIVAL GUIDE

EXAMS:

1 Write the answers on your wrist

2 Be ill

3 Write anything

Answers to puzzles on the previous page

Movie Quotes: Jennifer Cavillari Barret (Ali McGraw) *Love Story* (1970)

Where on Earth?: The West Indies   In Shape: 26.

Dominological: 0 at the top and 4 at the bottom; numbers at the top decrease by 2 and those at the bottom increase by one each time.

Pyramid Plus: A=8, B=15, C=5, D=3, E=14, F=23, G=20, H=8, I=17, J=43, K=28, L=25, M=71, N=53, O=124.

Who Am I?: Gordon Sumner (Sting)

Every oval shape contains a different letter from A to K inclusive. Use the clues to determine their locations. Reference in the clues to 'due' means in any location along the same horizontal or vertical line.

1 D is due north of and next to K, which is due west of H.

2 J is due north of and next to E, which is due west of I, which is due north of B.

3 C is due west of G, which is next to and due north of A, which is due south of F.

4 A is further west than I, which is further south than K.

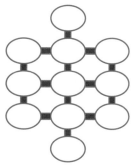

Today we are all going to:

Eat only bananas until next New Year's Day.

TWO-WORD HOROSCOPES

Aries – not you

Taurus – be yourself

Gemini – little pleasures

Cancer – why you?

Leo – work it!

Virgo – last gasp

Libra – in here

Scorpio – nosy neighbors

Sagittarius – new delights

Capricorn – last chance

Aquarius – lovely outfit

Pisces – big feet

DESIGN YOUR OWN

PRISON CELL

MY NEXT
PET

Animal:
_____

Name:
_____

Living Space:
_____

Answers to puzzles on the previous page

What Does It Mean?: Covered with dust
Brainteaser: Kariba
Letter Tracker: Greenland, Australia, Jamaica, Sicily, Iceland, Trinidad, Spitzbergen, Sardinia, Barbados, Madagascar, Sumatra, Sri Lanka, Cuba, Tenerife, Honshu, Crete.

Sum Total:

5	x	8	+	1
x		+		+
6	+	3	x	2
−		−		x
9	−	4	x	7

TOTAL CONCENTRATION

Can you fill in the missing numbers so that each row, each column and two longest diagonal lines meet the totals given?

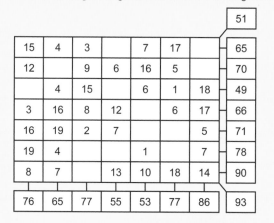

							51
15	4	3		7	17		65
12		9	6	16	5		70
	4	15		6	1	18	49
3	16	8	12		6	17	66
16	19	2	7			5	71
19	4			1		7	78
8	7		13	10	18	14	90
76	65	77	55	53	77	86	93

WORD LADDER

Change one letter at a time (but not the position of any letter) to make a new word – and move from the word at the top of the ladder to the word at the bottom using the exact number of rungs provided.

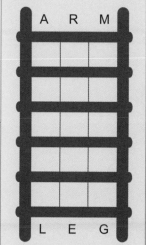

A R M

L E G

STARTING LINE

Which three-letter word can be placed at the start, to form three seven-letter words?

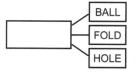

- BALL
- FOLD
- HOLE

WEATHER for OPTIMISTS

Today the weather will be:

Foggy, with zero visibility; but at least you won't be able to see anything unpleasant.

TIED UP AT PRESENT

Which boy is holding the string attached to the present?

TWO DOWN

Fit five of the seven listed words into the Across rows in the grid, so that the other two words read down the shaded columns numbered 2 and 3.

ADULT	ELDER
MELON	PRINT
SEAMY	SLEEP
	VENOM

1	2		3
4			
5			
6			
7			

PICK 'N' MIX

Choose three words to describe your ideal job:

Important	Management
Executive	Money
Useful	Controlling
Worthy	Fun
Travel	Easy

Answers to puzzles on the previous page

Elimination:

```
          D
     J    K    H
     E    F    I
     C    G    B
          A
```

113

CLOCKWORDS

It's a race against the clock…
How many common words of three or more different letters can you make from those on the clock face (without using plurals, proper nouns or abbreviations) in ten minutes? All words must contain BOTH the letters indicated by the hands on the clock.

QUOTE OF THE DAY

"I've had a wonderful evening, but this wasn't it."
Groucho Marx

WEATHER for PESSIMISTS

Today the weather will be:

Stormy, with huge scary hailstones

DICEY ARITHMETIC

Using three of the arithmetical signs ÷, −, x and +, can you achieve the correct total?

    =

BERMUDA TRIANGLE

Travel through the 'Bermuda Triangle' by visiting one room at a time and collecting a letter from each. You can enter the outside passageway as often as you like, but can only visit each room once. When you've completed your tour, the 15 letters spell out a word.

PROVERBS AND SAYINGS

The letters on the tiles were once all in place, but dropped out, falling in a straight line into the lower grid. Some tiles dropped earlier than others, so those on the lowest row aren't all from the same row in the grid above. Can you put them back into position in order to reveal a well-known proverb or saying?

I	A		N	E		B	R
I	T		N	O	U	E	S	T
R	T	I	P	S	V	R	U	.

JOIN THE DOTS

Answers to puzzles on the previous page

Total Concentration: From left to right, top to bottom the missing numbers are: 5, 14, 11, 11, 3, 2, 4, 9, 13, 20, 10, 17 and 20.

Word Ladder – One solution is: ARM, aim, dim, dig, big, beg, LEG.

Starting Line: PIN

Tied up at Present: Boy B

Two Down: Across: 1 Seamy, 4 Sleep, 5 Adult, 6 Venom, 7 Print. Down: 2 Elder, 3 Melon.

MISSING LINKS

Which word links the one on the left with the one on the right? We've done the first one, and when you've finished them all, the first letters of the link words will spell another word.

FUNNY	**BONE**	DRY
STAFF		MATE
HERE		NEATH
LANDING		FRIGHT
CART		TRADER

LETTER TRACKER

Begin in the central shaded square and follow a continuous path which will track from square to square, up, down and sideways, but never diagonally.

Your trail should cover every letter once only, in order to find:

Nineteen planets, stars and heavenly bodies.

R	P	P	U	L	D	A	R	S	P	I
I	O	O	S	A	E	B	A	N	A	C
A	L	N	A	C	T	H	M	S	P	L
T	A	R	I	S	R	R	E	U	T	U
L	A	S	U	R	A	C	E	N	O	S
A	R	C	T	U	E	U	V	U	T	A
S	E	R	E	T	I	R	Y	R	T	E
N	T	A	R	U	P	U	J	N	S	R
A	A	I	R	R	A	N	U	S	A	O
E	G	G	S	R	I	L	L	A	C	I
V	L	E	U	I	S	A	E	P	S	D

SWEET BAD MUSIC

So who on earth was responsible for this lyric?

"My panty line shows
Got a run in my hose
My hair went flat
Man, I hate that"

MISSING LETTERS

One letter of the alphabet is missing from each box. Find them all and place them in the order of the numbered boxes to reveal a six-letter word.

Word: _____

1	2	3
ULZAC	QYVMF	RAOFZ
MVBTE	RLNGS	KSPEX
DNWJS	HOWKT	GNTJB
KGOXH	XDUPC	HCIVD
QYIFR	EJZAB	YMUQW

4	5	6
VJIOA	YVCGJ	OITAN
HUBYG	BPKRS	SBJFM
FNWCP	LAUZE	PUCZD
TDKQR	HMDIF	QHVGL
SXMZE	NWTXQ	REYXK

Answers to puzzles on the previous page

Dicey Arithmetic: The signs are +, – and ÷.
Bermuda Triangle: DEMONSTRATIVELY
Proverbs and Sayings: It never rains but it pours.

BOX CLEVER

When the above is folded to form a cube, which one of the following can be produced?

A B C D E

WORDWHEEL

Using only the letters in the Wordwheel, you have ten minutes to find as many words as possible, none of which may be plurals, foreign words or proper nouns. Each word must be of three letters or more, all must contain the central letter and letters can only be used once in every word. There is at least one nine-letter word in the wheel.

Nine-letter word: _____

A H I N R C E P G

TOP TEN

ROADS ☐
LANES ☐
DRIVEWAYS ☐
HIGHWAYS ☐
TRACKS ☐
RIVERS ☐
CANALS ☐
PATHS ☐
WALKWAYS ☐
BRIDGES ☐

LAST MINUTE EXCUSES

In one minute, how many excuses can you find for:

Pointless relationships

CHARACTER ASSIGNATION

Fill in the answers to the clues, across the grid. Then read down the diagonal line of seven squares, to reveal:
The two-word name of a character created by George Eliot.

1
2
3
4
5
6
7
8

1 Former name of Zimbabwe
2 Terminated, stopped
3 Light-sensitive part of the eye
4 Tempest
5 Edible crustacean
6 Golf-ball support
7 Anno Domini
8 Vitamin, an important antioxidant

CHARACTER: _____

WHATEVER YOU DO, don't even THINK about...

Any of the following:

Greasy skin

Greasy hair

Greasy hands

SPELLING TEST

Which is the correctly spelled word?

RYTHM ☐

RHYTHM ☐

RYTHEM ☐

Answers to puzzles on the previous page

Missing Links: Bone, Room, Under, Stage, Horse.
Thus: BRUSH
Music Trivia: Suzanne Vega OR Rebecca Pidgeon (both answers are correct).
Letter Tracker: Earth, Mercury, Venus, Pluto, Saturn, Jupiter, Uranus, Asteroids, Capella, Sirius, Rigel, Vega, Antares, Arcturus, Altair, Polaris, Canopus, Aldebaran, Spica.
Sweet Bad Music: Shania Twain *Honey I'm Home*
Missing Letters: PILLOW

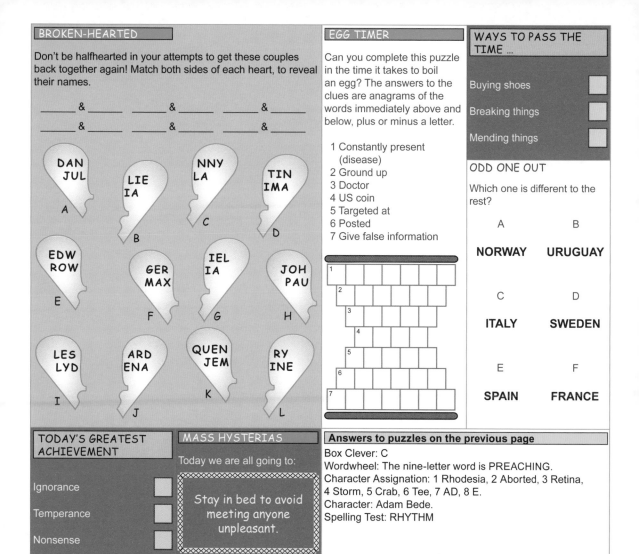

BROKEN-HEARTED

Don't be halfhearted in your attempts to get these couples back together again! Match both sides of each heart, to reveal their names.

_____ & _____ _____ & _____ _____ & _____
_____ & _____ _____ & _____ _____ & _____

DAN JUL
A

LIE IA
B

NNY LA
C

TIN IMA
D

EDW ROW
E

GER MAX
F

IEL IA
G

JOH PAU
H

LES LYD
I

ARD ENA
J

QUEN JEM
K

RY INE
L

EGG TIMER

Can you complete this puzzle in the time it takes to boil an egg? The answers to the clues are anagrams of the words immediately above and below, plus or minus a letter.

1 Constantly present (disease)
2 Ground up
3 Doctor
4 US coin
5 Targeted at
6 Posted
7 Give false information

WAYS TO PASS THE TIME ...

Buying shoes ☐

Breaking things ☐

Mending things ☐

ODD ONE OUT

Which one is different to the rest?

A **NORWAY**
B **URUGUAY**
C **ITALY**
D **SWEDEN**
E **SPAIN**
F **FRANCE**

TODAY'S GREATEST ACHIEVEMENT

Ignorance ☐

Temperance ☐

Nonsense ☐

MASS HYSTERIAS

Today we are all going to:

Stay in bed to avoid meeting anyone unpleasant.

Answers to puzzles on the previous page

Box Clever: C
Wordwheel: The nine-letter word is PREACHING.
Character Assignation: 1 Rhodesia, 2 Aborted, 3 Retina, 4 Storm, 5 Crab, 6 Tee, 7 AD, 8 E.
Character: Adam Bede.
Spelling Test: RHYTHM

ON THE TILES

In this puzzle, the eight tiles on the right must be fitted into the pattern in the middle so as to form four words reading across and five words reading down. No tile may be rotated!

LOOSE VOWELS

Someone has taken all the vowels out of what was once a completed crossword. Can you put them all back in again? You should use only those letters beneath the grid.

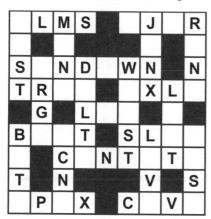

A A A A A A A A A A
E E E E E E E E E E
I I
O O O
U U U

A MATCHING PAIR

Which are the only two that are identical in every way?

A B

C D

E F

Answers to puzzles on the previous page

Broken-hearted: A and G, E and J, F and L, H and C, I and B, K and D.
Egg Timer: 1 Endemic, 2 Minced, 3 Medic, 4 Dime, 5 Aimed, 6 Mailed, 7 Mislead.
Odd One Out: B – It is the only country not in Europe.

DESIGN YOUR OWN
BATHROOM

PAIR SHAPES

In the box below there are shapes in three different colors, red, white and blue. Any shape may have been rotated, but can you see which is the only shape to appear exactly twice in exactly the same color?

REAL WORDS

Which is the real word?

Mugdemp ☐

Mugdint ☐

Magadis ☐

STARTER LETTER

Write down one each of the listed items, all of which must begin with the starter letter:

L

Country	
Tree	
Boy's name	
Girl's name	
River	
City	
Animal	
Make of car	
Drink	

CROSSED WORDS

Using only the letters above the diagram, fill in the squares to make a common two-word phrase, one word reading down and the other across.

A E E N P T T

		S	

PRE-FAME NAME GAME

By what name do we know this famous person? ☆

Lesley Hornby

WHAT DOES IT MEAN?

What is the meaning of the word

Floccinaucinihilipilification

Answer: _____

_____

119

CODEWORD

This is a crossword puzzle in code. Every number represents a different letter of the alphabet and this number remains the same throughout the puzzle. Use the letters either side of the grid as well as the check-box below the grid to keep a track on your progress.

A
B
C
D
E
F
G
H
I
J
K
L
M

N
O
P
Q
R
S
T
U
V
W
X
Y
Z

1	2	3	4	5	6	7	8	9	10	11	12	13
						A						

14	15	16	17	18	19	20	21	22	23	24	25	26
						R					C	

A IS TO B

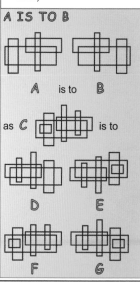

A is to B

as C is to

D   E

F   G

ARRANGING THINGS

If you fit six of these seven words into the grid, the word left over will appear reading down the shaded squares.

ACUMEN   AFRAID
OPPOSE   SCRAWL
SHIELD   THROWN
TOMATO

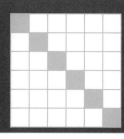

EYE-SPY

I spy with my little eye something beginning with:

E

_____

MIRROR WRITING

Write this word upside down:

PLASTIC

_____

DO YOU KNOW...

...what happened medically on this date?

11 January 1922

PRE-FAME NAME GAME

By what name do we know this famous person?

Harvey Lee Yeary

_____

COMPLETE THIS LIMERICK:

A model, whilst walking in rain

Was so slim, she got washed down a drain

And was swept out to sea

Shouting "Oh, rescue me!"

_____

SWEET BAD MUSIC

So who on earth was responsible for this lyric?

"I don't think that I've got the stomach
To stomach calling you today"

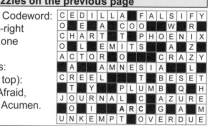

DOMINADDITION

Can you place the remaining dominoes in their correct positions, so that the total number of spots in each of the four rows and five columns equals the sum at the end of that row or column?

= 16
= 21
= 15
= 22

= 13 = 16 = 18 = 10 = 17

WHO AM I?

Large fat noise

I am:

_____

Answers to puzzles on the previous page

A is to B: G – They are left-right mirror images of one another.

Arranging Things:
Across (from the top): Tomato, Shield, Afraid, Oppose, Scrawl, Acumen.
Down: Thrown.

Codeword:

C	E	D	I	L	L	A		F	A	L	S	I	F	Y
O		E		A		C	O	O			W		R	
C	H	A	R	T		T		P	H	O	E	N	I	X
O		L		E	M	I	T	S			A		Z	
A	C	T	O	R		O			C	R	A	Z	Y	
	A			A	M	N	E	S	I	A			L	
C	R	E	E	L			T		B	E	S	E	T	
T		Y			P	L	U	M	B		Q		H	
J	O	U	R	N	A	L		C		A	Z	U	R	E
O		I		A	R	C		G			A		M	
U	N	K	E	M	P	T		O	V	E	R	D	U	E

121

TWO-WORD HOROSCOPES

Aries – big deal

Taurus – not today

Gemini – tell him!

Cancer – silver lining

Leo – leave it

Virgo – grow up

Libra – give up

Scorpio – pipe down

Sagittarius – cuddle time

Capricorn – top notch

Aquarius – what now?

Pisces – next time

SHAPE RECOGNITION

Which are the only three pieces which will fit together to form a copy of this black shape?

A B C D

E F

H G

I J

SECRET MISSION

Your secret mission (should you choose to accept it) is:

To bring down the government of a small Latin American country using only string.

REAL WORDS

Which is the real word?

Octonocity ☐

Orphrey ☐

Octobucculus ☐

NAMED AND SHAMED

Sex pest

_____

Tailspin

_____

Crooked

_____

HEXAGONY

Can you place the hexagons in the grid, so that where any triangle touches another along a straight line, the contents of both are the same? One triangle is already filled.

PRE-FAME NAME GAME

By what name do we know this famous person?

Marion Michael Morrison

_____

MUSIC TRIVIA

Who had a solo hit in 1993 with *Living on My Own*?

SNAKES AND LADDERS

This is a standard game, so when you land at the foot of a ladder, you climb it; and when you land on the head of a snake, you slide down its tail. You need to throw an exact number to land on 100 to win – counting backwards if you don't, eg if you land on 98 and throw a five, you will end up on 97. The dice is thrown for you and always lands in this recurring order: 2, 5, 6, 1, 4, 3, so you can start by immediately placing your counter on square 2. Good luck – hope you win!

100	99	98	97	96	95	94	93	92	91
81	82	83	84	85	86	87	88	89	90
80	79	78	77	76	75	74	73	72	71
61	62	63	64	65	66	67	68	69	70
60	59	58	57	56	55	54	53	52	51
41	42	43	44	45	46	47	48	49	50
40	39	38	37	36	35	34	33	32	31
21	22	23	24	25	26	27	28	29	30
20	19	18	17	16	15	14	13	12	11
1	2	3	4	5	6	7	8	9	10

TANGLED TACKLE

Which of these anglers has landed the fish?

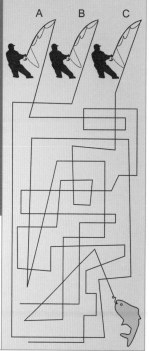

A   B   C

PATCHWORK

Fit the letters A, B, C, D, E and F into the grid below, so that every horizontal row, every vertical column and every shape of six smaller squares contain six different letters. Some are already in place.

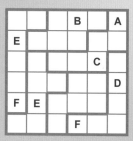

MOVIE QUOTES

We give you a line, you tell us who said it and the film:

"My precious."

WHERE ON EARTH?

Where on Earth is Tittybong?

Answer: _____

QUOTE OF THE DAY

"Those who dance are considered insane by those who cannot hear the music."
George Carlin

Answers to puzzles on the previous page

Shape Recognition:
D, F and G
Real Words: Orphrey
Pre-fame Name Game: John Wayne
Music Trivia: Freddie Mercury

Hexagony:

DICE-SECTION

Printed onto every one of the six numbered dice below are six letters (one per side), which can be rearranged to form the answer to each clue; however, some sides are invisible to you. Use the clues and write every answer into the grid. When correctly filled, the letters in the shaded squares, reading in the order 1 to 6, will spell out a season of the year.

1 Tiny amount

2 Light wind, breeze

3 Lebanese capital

4 The East

5 Trumpet-like instrument

6 East Mediterranean sea

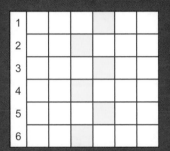

WEATHER for OPTIMISTS

Today the weather will be:

Nondescript, but you could hope for a beautiful sunset.

TOP TEN

RUN	
WALK	
CRAWL	
SKIP	
JUMP	
LEAP	
HOP	
STROLL	
CREEP	
JOG	

ON TARGET

The answers to the clues read from the outer circle to the center, all ending with the same letter. When you've finished, the letters in the shaded ring will give a word.

1 Animal viscera

2 Bore (into)

3 Inland waterway

4 Heavenly being

5 Suppress, appease

6 Month; also a girl's name

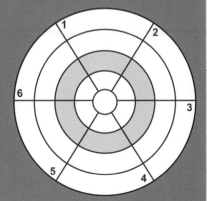

BRAINTEASER

Which is the largest country in the world with only one time zone?

Answers to puzzles on the previous page

Tangled Tackle: Angler B
Movie Quotes: Gollum (Andy Serkis)
The Lord of the Rings: The Two Towers (2002)
Where on Earth?: Australia

Patchwork:

C	D	F	B	E	A
E	A	D	C	B	F
A	F	E	D	C	B
B	C	A	E	F	D
F	E	B	A	D	C
D	B	C	F	A	E

WHATEVER NEXT?

Which of the numbered alternatives comes next in this sequence:

P	K	R	M	T	?

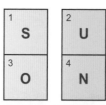

1   S

2   U

3   O

4   N

COUPLINGS

Apart from two, every word listed below can be coupled with one of the others to make another word or phrase. Rearrange the letters of the two which can't be paired together to form one word, the name of a large seabird.

1 DRIVER	2 SOUTH
3 NATIONAL	4 BOSS
5 TALK	6 BREAK
7 OPENER	8 ALTAR
9 POLE	10 SCREW
11 PILLOW	12 ANTHEM
13 AWAY	14 CAN

Answer: _____

WEATHER for PESSIMISTS

Today the weather will be:

Snowing so hard it will cause an avalanche, burying your house

GET THE LOOK

Make the face:

NAUGHTY

PICK 'N' MIX

Choose three words to create your favorite meal:

Ground Meat   Eggs
Tomatoes   Peas
Sweetcorn   Bacon
Lamb Chops   Lettuce
Bread   Butter

UNLIKELY CANDIDATE

TALK SHOW HOST

_____

JIGSAW CROSSWORD

Fit the blocks into the empty grid to form a complete crossword which, when finished, will be symmetrical, similar to the example seen here:

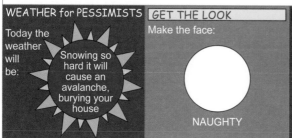

Answers to puzzles on the previous page

On Target: 1 Offal, 2 Drill, 3 Canal, 4 Angel, 5 Quell, 6 April. The word is: FINGER

Brainteaser: China (it actually spans five zones).

Dice-Section:

M	O	R	S	E	L
Z	E	P	H	Y	R
B	E	I	R	U	T
O	R	I	E	N	T
C	O	R	N	E	T
A	E	G	E	A	N

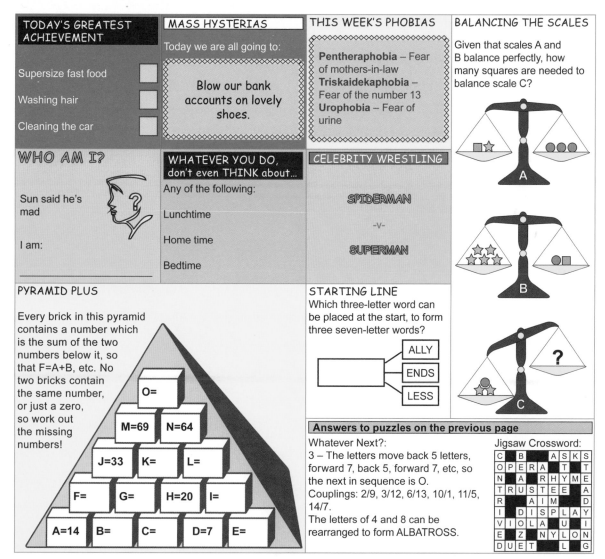

TODAY'S GREATEST ACHIEVEMENT

Supersize fast food ☐

Washing hair ☐

Cleaning the car ☐

MASS HYSTERIAS

Today we are all going to:

Blow our bank accounts on lovely shoes.

THIS WEEK'S PHOBIAS

Pentheraphobia – Fear of mothers-in-law
Triskaidekaphobia – Fear of the number 13
Urophobia – Fear of urine

BALANCING THE SCALES

Given that scales A and B balance perfectly, how many squares are needed to balance scale C?

WHO AM I?

Sun said he's mad

I am: _____

WHATEVER YOU DO, don't even THINK about...

Any of the following:

Lunchtime

Home time

Bedtime

CELEBRITY WRESTLING

SPIDERMAN

–v–

SUPERMAN

PYRAMID PLUS

Every brick in this pyramid contains a number which is the sum of the two numbers below it, so that F=A+B, etc. No two bricks contain the same number, or just a zero, so work out the missing numbers!

O=

M=69 N=64

J=33 K= L=

F= G= H=20 I=

A=14 B= C= D=7 E=

STARTING LINE

Which three-letter word can be placed at the start, to form three seven-letter words?

[ ] — ALLY
      ENDS
      LESS

Answers to puzzles on the previous page

Whatever Next?:
3 – The letters move back 5 letters, forward 7, back 5, forward 7, etc, so the next in sequence is O.
Couplings: 2/9, 3/12, 6/13, 10/1, 11/5, 14/7.
The letters of 4 and 8 can be rearranged to form ALBATROSS.

Jigsaw Crossword:

C		B			A	S	K	S
O	P	E	R	A		T		T
N		A		R	H	Y	M	E
T	R	U	S	T	E	E		A
R			A	I	M			D
I		D	I	S	P	L	A	Y
V	I	O	L	A		U		I
E		Z		N	Y	L	O	N
D	U	E	T			L		G

126

WAYS TO PASS THE TIME ...

Slicing cucumbers ☐

Trying ☐

Training ☐

WORDFILLER

Can you place all the listed words into the grid below?

3 letters	5 letters		7 letters
Egg	Amuse	Essay	Example
Pat	Cadet	Gnarl	Hostess
	Chaos	Group	
4 letters	Clamp	Halve	
Also	Cocoa	Liner	9 letters
Lump	Cycle	Mural	Stimulate
Salt	Early	Nanny	
Toga	Enemy	Sinus	
	Ensue	Syria	

SUDOKU

The numbers from 1 to 9 inclusive need to be placed into the grid below in such a way that every horizontal row and vertical column contains nine different digits. In addition, each of the nine blocks of nine smaller squares should also contain nine different numbers. The clues are the numbers already placed.

	5	1		7				3
		8		3	6	7	4	
			9			2	6	5
2			7	4				
1	4						3	8
				1	3			2
4	6	5			8			
	3	9	2	6		1		
7				5		8	9	

Answers to puzzles on the previous page

Balancing the Scales: 1
Who Am I?: Saddam Hussein
Pyramid Plus: A=14, B=3, C=13, D=7, E=1, F=17, G=16, H=20, I=8, J=33, K=36, L=28, M=69, N=64, O=133.
Starting Line: LEG

JOIN THE DOTS

THIS WEEK'S PHOBIAS

Motorphobia – Fear of automobiles
Pediculophobia – Fear of lice
Peladophobia – Fear of bald people

JUST A WORD

Can you find 'MILK' hidden in the grid, wordsearch-style?

```
M T E K I L R N M C E L M
I C M I K T S M T R L I T
E K K L M E I S I C M S K
M R I M O N M K E K T M E
S M L R N T E L I M S C I
M S R K I M C L O O E R M
```

MOVIE QUOTES

We give you a line, you tell us who said it and the film:

"Nobody puts Baby in a corner."

WHERE ON HEARTHI ?

Where on Earth is Turdo?

Answer: _____

SYMBOLISM

What whole number value between 1 and 9 should be allocated to each different symbol in order to reach the sum totals shown at the end of each row and column?

■	●	▲	◆	=21
●	▲	●	◆	=22
◆	■	●	●	=24
▲	■	■	▲	=26

=21 =27 =28 =17

CROSSED WORDS

Using only the letters above the diagram, fill in the squares to make a common two-word phrase, one word reading down and the other across.

E E H L M T V Y

(crossword grid with letter A)

NEWSWORTHY

Fill this newspaper spread with worthy stories and pictures of your own…

Answers to puzzles on the previous page

Wordfiller:

```
H O S T E S S   E N E M Y
A   I   A   T O G A   U
L I N E R   I   G N A R L
V   U   L U M P   N   A
E S S A Y   U   C Y C L E
Y   M   A L S O   L   N
G R O U P   A   C H A O S
  I   S A L T   O   M   U
C A D E T   E X A M P L E
```

Sudoku:

6	5	1	4	7	2	9	8	3
9	2	8	5	3	6	7	4	1
3	7	4	9	8	1	2	6	5
2	8	3	7	4	5	6	1	9
1	4	7	6	2	9	5	3	8
5	9	6	8	1	3	4	7	2
4	6	5	1	9	8	3	2	7
8	3	9	2	6	7	1	5	4
7	1	2	3	5	4	8	9	6

DELETIONS

There are 11 birds and a proverb hidden in this grid. Taking one letter from each box, cross off the six-letter birds in the Across rows. Do the same for the five-letter birds in the Down columns. When you have finished, the letters remaining will reveal the proverb reading from left-to-right and row by row.

ACROSS

1 _____
2 _____
3 _____
4 _____
5 _____

DOWN

1 _____
2 _____
3 _____
4 _____
5 _____
6 _____

	1	2	3	4	5	6
1	SOT	OQS	PDR	SRO	NME	YOR
2	TWM	UAH	AIG	NPT	IAG	OIE
3	ITS	TAH	VRH	UEO	CSW	BAH
4	YCF	OIT	EON	BDR	OAE	INR
5	ETO	TLA	GHN	KLI	NWE	TNG

TWO DOWN

Fit five of the seven listed words into the Across rows in the grid, so that the other two words read down the shaded columns numbered 2 and 3.

KNOWN   MINOR
PRINT   SNOWY
SPIKE   STING
      TRUNK

1	2		3	
4				
5				
6				
7				

NUMB-SKULL

Fit the listed numbers into the grid, crossword-fashion.

3 digits
552
731
918
985

4 digits
1627
1718
2444
4316
4627
5967
6574
7271
7765
8868
8937
9064

5 digits
17394
36364
39056
51382
65525
75414
87567
95200

7 digits
5380209
8576126

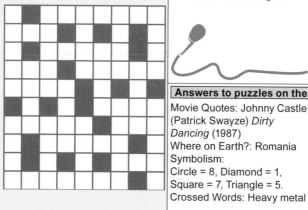

MUSIC TRIVIA

Genie in a Bottle was a No 1 hit for which singer?

Answers to puzzles on the previous page

Movie Quotes: Johnny Castle (Patrick Swayze) *Dirty Dancing* (1987)
Where on Earth?: Romania
Symbolism:
Circle = 8, Diamond = 1, Square = 7, Triangle = 5.
Crossed Words: Heavy metal

Just a Word:

M	T	E	K	I	L	R	N	M	C	E	L	M
I	C	M	I	**K**	T	S	M	T	R	L	I	T
E	K	K	**L**	M	E	I	S	I	C	M	S	K
M	R	**I**	M	O	N	M	K	E	K	T	M	E
S	**M**	L	R	N	T	E	L	I	M	S	C	I
M	S	R	K	I	M	C	L	O	O	E	R	M

BOX CLEVER

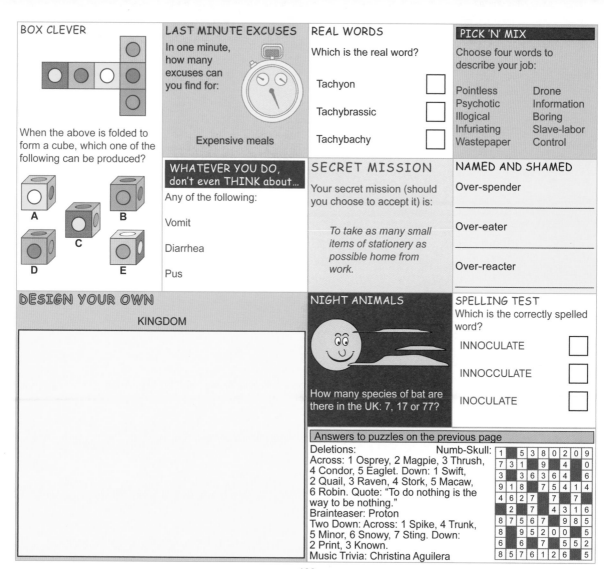

When the above is folded to form a cube, which one of the following can be produced?

A B C D E

LAST MINUTE EXCUSES

In one minute, how many excuses can you find for:

Expensive meals

REAL WORDS

Which is the real word?

Tachyon ☐

Tachybrassic ☐

Tachybachy ☐

PICK 'N' MIX

Choose four words to describe your job:

Pointless   Drone
Psychotic   Information
Illogical   Boring
Infuriating   Slave-labor
Wastepaper   Control

WHATEVER YOU DO, don't even THINK about...

Any of the following:

Vomit

Diarrhea

Pus

SECRET MISSION

Your secret mission (should you choose to accept it) is:

To take as many small items of stationery as possible home from work.

NAMED AND SHAMED

Over-spender
_____

Over-eater
_____

Over-reacter
_____

DESIGN YOUR OWN

KINGDOM

NIGHT ANIMALS

How many species of bat are there in the UK: 7, 17 or 77?

SPELLING TEST
Which is the correctly spelled word?

INNOCULATE ☐

INNOCCULATE ☐

INOCULATE ☐

Answers to puzzles on the previous page

Deletions:
Across: 1 Osprey, 2 Magpie, 3 Thrush, 4 Condor, 5 Eaglet. Down: 1 Swift, 2 Quail, 3 Raven, 4 Stork, 5 Macaw, 6 Robin. Quote: "To do nothing is the way to be nothing."
Brainteaser: Proton
Two Down: Across: 1 Spike, 4 Trunk, 5 Minor, 6 Snowy, 7 Sting. Down: 2 Print, 3 Known.
Music Trivia: Christina Aguilera

Numb-Skull:

1		5	3	8	0	2	0	9
7	3	1		9		4		0
3		3	6	3	6	4		6
9	1	8		7	5	4	1	4
4	6	2	7		7		7	
	2		7		4	3	1	6
8	7	5	6	7		9	8	5
8		9	5	2	0	0		5
6		6		7		5	5	2
8	5	7	6	1	2	6		5

KEYWORD

Simply fill in the letters missing from the different words numbered 1-6 and enter them into the numbered boxes, to reveal the hidden keyword. Take care, however, as some may have more than one possible letter which could fit: for example S — M E might be either SAME or SOME.

| 1 | 2 | 3 | 4 | 5 | 6 |

1 SWAM—   2 DEE—ED

3 —ALMED   4 CLO—K

5 PANE—   6 DR—WN

WORDSEARCH

Can you find all of the listed fun words in the grid? Words may run in either a forwards or backwards direction, horizontally, vertically or diagonally, but always in a straight, uninterrupted line.

AMUSE

BEGUILE

CHARM

CHEER

DECEIVE

DELIGHT

DISPORT

DIVERT

ENLIVEN

ENTERTAIN

FROLIC

```
D V X T N E M I R R E M X
G M P L A Y N M L E B W E
N R T S W X H L Z T L A H
O A M U S E C E I U W A N
I H M W C H I E M V J J X
T C W P E F L L Z D E D T
A P T E U I O E V I N N M
E D R N U U R M S V T L Y
R D I G Y M F M I E E O L
C R E S P T I F E R R V E
E B C C P L H I X T T M V
R W L O E O E R D Z A H I
X W Z B N I R A I G I V L
E L A U G H V T S L N F G
D L T H G I L E D E L W L
```

FUN	MERRIMENT	RECREATION
GAME	MIRTH	RELAX
LAUGH	PLAY	SMILE
LIVELY	PLEASE	THRILL

TOP FIVE

Best colors to wear:

1 _____

2 _____

_____

_____

3 _____

_____

4 _____

_____

5 _____

_____

SWEET BAD MUSIC

So who on earth was responsible for this lyric?

"Your butt is mine"

SIMPLE AS A,B,C

In the grid, each row across, column down and diagonal line of six squares should contain two each of A, B and C. The clues relate to the squares only in that row or column. We give as many clues as we think you need (including any letters already in the grid), so can you place the letters correctly?

Across:
1 The As are further right than the Cs.
2 The As are between the Bs.
5 Any three adjacent squares contain three different letters.
6 The As are further right than the Cs.

Down:
1 The Bs are lower than the Cs.
2 The Cs are lower than the Bs.
3 The As are higher than the Bs.
5 One A is directly next to and below a B, and the other is directly next to and below a C. However, no B is directly next to and below a C.

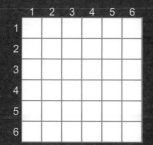

WORD LADDER

Change one letter at a time (but not the position of any letter) to make a new word – and move from the word at the top of the ladder to the word at the bottom using the exact number of rungs provided.

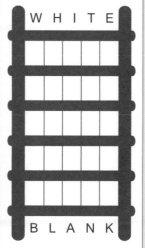

W H I T E

B L A N K

GOOD IMPRESSIONS

Can you pair up these door keys with the impressions of their ends?

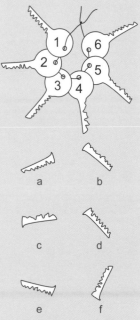

a

b

c

d

e

f

PRE-FAME NAME GAME

By what name do we know this famous person?

Annie Mae Bullock

ALL AT SEA

The Black Pig was a ship belonging to which fictional character?

132

LEADING LADIES

Which of these women is walking the dog?

A

B

C

DO YOU KNOW...

...what happened on this date?

22 November 1963

WHAT DOES IT MEAN?

What is the meaning of the word

Nudiustertian

Answer: _____

_____

WHAT'S IN A NAME?

How many words (other names included) can you make from the name:

ALEXANDER

_____

_____

_____

_____

SUM THOUGHTS

What is the sum total of all of the following two-digit numbers?

39

61

56

14

41

15

84

USE YOUR IMAGINATION

Can you fill each of these boxes with a different flower?

WEATHER for OPTIMISTS

Today the weather will be:

Rainy; clouds will burst periodically, so catch a shower and have a rain dance.

Answers to puzzles on the previous page

Word Ladder – One solution is: WHITE, whine, chine, chink, clink, blink, BLANK.

Good Impressions: 1-d, 2-f, 3-e, 4-c, 5-b, 6-a.

Pre-fame Name Game: Tina Turner

All at Sea: Captain Pugwash

Simple as A,B,C:

C	B	C	A	B	A
C	B	A	C	A	B
B	A	A	C	B	C
A	A	B	B	C	C
A	C	B	A	C	B
B	C	C	B	A	A

ON THE TILES

In this puzzle, the eight tiles on the right must be fitted into the pattern in the middle so as to form four words reading across and five words reading down. No tile may be rotated!

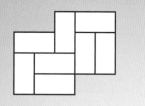

W O	Y	A
E D	E	N
	E W	
L F		
K L	R A	

WEATHER for PESSIMISTS

Today the weather will be:

Extremely warm, with the risk of heat stroke

AMAZING

Can you work your way from the entrance at the top to the exit at the bottom of this maze?

ROUNDWORD

Write the answer to each clue in a clockwise direction. Every solution overlaps the next by either one, two or three letters and each solution starts in its numbered section.

The solution to the final clue ends with the letter in the first square.

1 Slim, thin
2 Ridicule
3 Early stages
4 Sicilian volcano
5 Cold region
6 Aquatic reptile
7 Wanders off course

WHO AM I?

An oral danger

I am:

_____

SECRET MISSION

Your secret mission (should you choose to accept it) is:

To guide the benevolent aliens to a safe landing place.

STARTING LINE

Which three-letter word can be placed at the start, to form three seven-letter words?

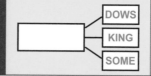

DOWS

KING

SOME

MUSIC TRIVIA

Which British singer was known as the White Lady of Soul?

GET THE LOOK

Make the face:

BORED

IN CHAINS

This chain of letters contains the names of three vegetables. The letters are in the correct order but need to be picked out.

PRAUOTRAKBSANRGIAPA

_____   _____

_____

CROSSWISE

Rearrange the six scrambled groups of letters to form words and then decide where each fits in the grid. Some letters are already in place.

AACNTV   CEIKNS
DEEISV   DEISST
EEKRSW   ENSSTU

WHOLESOME FUN

In this puzzle, you need to find a five-letter word by deciding which common letter has been removed from the trios of words on each line.

Enter that letter into the circle at the end of each row and the word will be revealed reading downwards.

_OAT	PA_T	EPI_	◯
ECH_	B_IL	H_ST	◯
P_IL	SW_Y	B_CK	◯
U_ER	_ACK	ALA_	◯
_RIP	PAS_	S_OP	◯

LAST MINUTE EXCUSES

In one minute, how many excuses can you find for:

Fast sports cars

Answers to puzzles on the previous page

On the Tiles:

		F	E	D
R	A	L	L	Y
A	W	O	K	E
N	E	W		

Roundword: 1 Slender, 2 Derision, 3 Onset, 4 Etna, 5 Arctic, 6 Crocodile, 7 Errs.

Amazing:

135

TOP TEN

PIES

CAKES

COOKIES

JELLIES

TRIFLES

MERINGUES

ICE CREAMS

PUDDINGS

PASTRIES

TARTS

SPOT THE SAME

Only two of these modern abstract paintings are identical in every way: which?

NUMBER BOX

In this puzzle, simply use the hints given to enter nine different numbers 1-9 in their correct boxes.

7 is next to and left of 5
3 is next to and below 9
8 is two squares below 5
1 is two squares right of 4
6 is two squares below 2

THE NAME GAME

Can you complete the six words reading across in such a way as to reveal the name of a well-known person in the shaded columns?

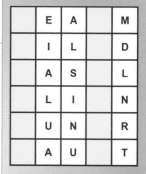

	E	A		M
	I	L		D
	A	S		L
	L	I		N
	U	N		R
	A	U		T

ON TARGET

The answers to the clues read from the outer circle to the center, all ending with the same letter. When you've finished, the letters in the shaded ring will give a word.

1 Periodic extraterrestrial body

2 Shoreline

3 Top-ranking

4 Prejudiced person

5 Wring

6 Claude ___, French painter (1840-1926)

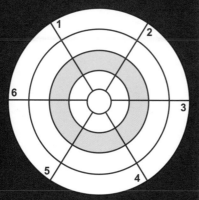

NIGHT ANIMALS

Which nocturnal creature is linked to a TV broadcasting network?

Answers to puzzles on the previous page

Who Am I?: Ronald Reagan
Starting Line: WIN
Music Trivia: Dusty Springfield
In Chains: Parsnip, Rutabaga and Okra.
Wholesome Fun: COAST

Crosswise:

D	E	S	I	S	T
E		I		U	
V	A	C	A	N	T
I		K		S	
S	K	E	W	E	R
E		N		T	

136

TOP FIVE

Best songs for a 21st, 30th or 40th birthday:

1 _____
2 _____
3 _____
4 _____
5 _____

CELEBRITY WRESTLING

SIGMUND FREUD

-v-

ANDREA DWORKIN

UNFINISHED PICTURE

Can you complete this doodle?

QUOTE OF THE DAY

"I am free of all prejudices. I hate everyone equally."

W C Fields

UNLIKELY CANDIDATE

BRAIN SURGEON

_____

DO YOU KNOW...

...what ended in fire on this date?

19 April 1993

JIGSAW CROSSWORD

Fit the blocks into the empty grid to form a complete crossword which, when finished, will be symmetrical, similar to the example seen here:

NAMED AND SHAMED

Insipid

_____

Insane

_____

Incensed

_____

MOVIE QUOTES

We give you a line, you tell us who said it and the film:

"I see dead people."

WHERE ON EARTH?

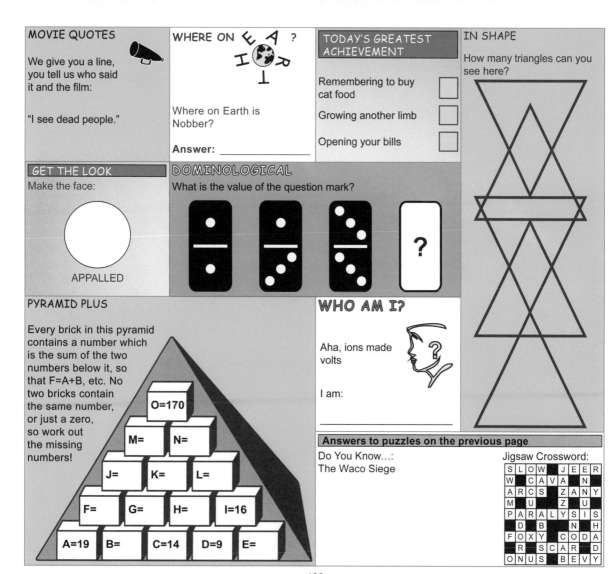

Where on Earth is Nobber?

Answer: _____

TODAY'S GREATEST ACHIEVEMENT

Remembering to buy cat food ☐

Growing another limb ☐

Opening your bills ☐

IN SHAPE

How many triangles can you see here?

GET THE LOOK

Make the face:

APPALLED

DOMINOLOGICAL

What is the value of the question mark?

?

PYRAMID PLUS

Every brick in this pyramid contains a number which is the sum of the two numbers below it, so that F=A+B, etc. No two bricks contain the same number, or just a zero, so work out the missing numbers!

O=170

M=   N=

J=   K=   L=

F=   G=   H=   I=16

A=19   B=   C=14   D=9   E=

WHO AM I?

Aha, ions made volts

I am:

_____

138

WHAT DOES IT MEAN?

What is the meaning of the word

Phenakism

Answer: _____

_____

BRAINTEASER

What were lost by King John, melted down by Oliver Cromwell and almost stolen by Thomas Blood?

WAYS TO PASS THE TIME …

Fighting ☐

Eating carrots ☐

Ignoring everything ☐

THIS WEEK'S PHOBIAS

Geliophobia – Fear of laughter

Myrmecophobia – Fear of ants

Ochophobia – Fear of being in a moving automobile

LETTER TRACKER

Begin in the central shaded square and follow a continuous path which will track from square to square, up, down and sideways, but never diagonally.

Your trail should cover every letter once only, in order to find:

Seventeen rivers of the world.

M	A	Z	O	N	N	I	L	E	R	A
A	O	L	K	E	B	E	U	P	H	T
Y	N	D	A	N	U	N	A	O	I	E
D	D	S	N	A	L	O	D	G	R	S
D	I	E	G	G	O	R	R	R	D	E
A	K	E	R	I	C	A	O	A	N	R
W	R	B	U	S	I	D	J	N	I	H
A	A	H	O	S	M	O	A	E	Y	A
R	R	M	A	P	U	T	R	T	G	N
S	I	H	T	S	D	O	C	S	E	O
E	M	A	N	O	U	H	O	N	I	R

SUM TOTAL

Place the digits 1-9, one per square, so that the sums are correct, according to the totals at the ends of the rows and columns. The calculations should be done in the order in which they appear, for example 6–2x5=20 should be read as 6–2(=4), then 4x5=20.

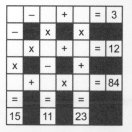

SECRET MISSION

Your secret mission (should you choose to accept it) is:

To erect a sign outside your home declaring it to be a radioactive site.

BRIEF SURVIVAL GUIDE

STARTING A NEW JOB:
1 Aim to get there on the specified day
2 Try to remember what you are supposed to be doing
3 Don't wear sequins or feathers (unless you are a stripper)

Answers to puzzles on the previous page

Movie Quotes: Cole Sear (Haley Joel Osment) *The Sixth Sense* (1999)

Where on Earth?: Donegal, Ireland   In Shape: 14.

Dominological: 3 at the top and 5 at the bottom; the face value increase by two each time, with the two added to the top and bottom halves alternately.

Pyramid Plus: A=19, B=6, C=14, D=9, E=7, F=25, G=20, H=23, I=16, J=45, K=43, L=39, M=88, N=82, O=170.

Who Am I?: Thomas Alva Edison

ELIMINATION

Every oval shape contains a different letter from A to K inclusive. Use the clues to determine their locations. Reference in the clues to 'due' means in any location along the same horizontal or vertical line.

1 A is due north of F and due west of E.

2 J is due north of G and due west of D.

3 C is due west of H, which is next to and due north of I.

4 B is next to and due north of K, which is further north than both D and E.

5 F is further east than G.

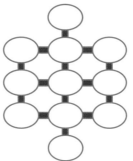

TWO-WORD HOROSCOPES

Aries – lost plot

Taurus – funny hours

Gemini – don't worry

Cancer – here today...

Leo – keep away

Virgo – buy shoes

Libra – show off

Scorpio – quite stupid

Sagittarius – torn pants

Capricorn – get them!

Aquarius – get ready...

Pisces – isolated incident

DESIGN YOUR OWN

TRAILER

MY NEXT HAIRDO

Style:

_____

Color:

_____

Length:

_____

Answers to puzzles on the previous page

What Does It Mean?: Deception or trickery.

Brainteaser: The British Crown Jewels

Letter Tracker: Colorado, Missouri, Ganges, Danube, Klondike, Brahmaputra, Jordan, Euphrates, Rio Grande, Rhine, Yangtse, Orinoco, Hudson, Thames, Irrawaddy, Amazon, Nile.

Sum Total:

6	–	5	+	2
–		x		x
1	x	4	+	8
x		–		+
3	+	9	x	7

TOTAL CONCENTRATION

Can you fill in the missing numbers so that each row, each column and two longest diagonal lines meet the totals given?

							70
13		18	3	12	6	1	60
8	3				11	14	73
4	9	6		13	17	10	69
11	19	15		20	6		97
	4	8	11	3			49
20	7	2	12	5		4	68
13		10	19	14		5	75
84	51	68	92	75	77	44	65

WORD LADDER

Change one letter at a time (but not the position of any letter) to make a new word – and move from the word at the top of the ladder to the word at the bottom using the exact number of rungs provided.

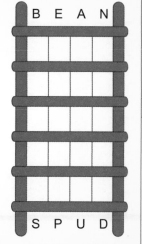

B E A N

S P U D

STARTING LINE

Which three-letter word can be placed at the start, to form three seven-letter words?

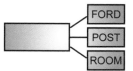

FORD

POST

ROOM

WEATHER for OPTIMISTS

Today the weather will be:

Freezing, with icicles which remind you of crystal chandeliers.

PICK 'N' MIX

Choose three words to describe a perfect holiday:

Sun	Sea
Sex	Food
Tent	Alcohol
Cottage	Activity
Hotel	Beach

TIED UP AT PRESENT

Which boy is holding the string attached to the present?

A B C

TWO DOWN

Fit five of the seven listed words into the Across rows in the grid, so that the other two words read down the shaded columns numbered 2 and 3.

ACUTE	BOUND
ENTER	FOCUS
OFFER	SUPER
USURP	

1	2		3	
4				
5				
6				
7				

Answers to puzzles on the previous page

Elimination:

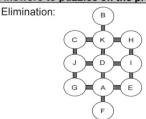

141

CLOCKWORDS

It's a race against the clock… How many common words of three or more different letters can you make from those on the clock face (without using plurals, proper nouns or abbreviations) in ten minutes? All words must contain BOTH the letters indicated by the hands on the clock.

WEATHER for PESSIMISTS

Today the weather will be:

Vicious, with temperatures you've never experienced

DICEY ARITHMETIC

Using three of the arithmetical signs ÷, −, x and +, can you achieve the correct total?

    =

BERMUDA TRIANGLE

Travel through the 'Bermuda Triangle' by visiting one room at a time and collecting a letter from each. You can enter the outside passageway as often as you like, but can only visit each room once. When you've completed your tour, the 15 letters spell out a word.

PROVERBS AND SAYINGS

The letters on the tiles were once all in place, but dropped out, falling in a straight line into the lower grid. Some tiles dropped earlier than others, so those on the lowest row aren't all from the same row in the grid above. Can you put them back into position in order to reveal a well-known proverb or saying?

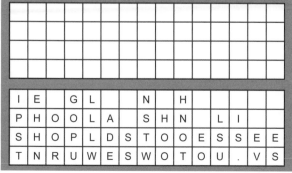

JOIN THE DOTS

Answers to puzzles on the previous page

Total Concentration: From left to right, top to bottom the missing numbers are: 7, 9, 20, 8, 10, 17, 9, 15, 7, 1, 18, 2 and 12.

Word Ladder – One solution is: BEAN, bead, dead, deed, seed, sped, SPUD.

Starting Line: BED

Tied up at Present: Boy C

Two Down: Across: 1 Offer, 4 Bound, 5 Acute, 6 Super, 7 Usurp. Down: 2 Focus, 3 Enter.

MISSING LINKS

Which word links the one on the left with the one on the right? We've done the first one, and when you've finished them all, the first letters of the link words will spell another word.

BLUE	**SKY**	LARK
ROCK		WOOD
ROLL		DRIVE
FRESH		FORCE
MOON		BULB

MUSIC TRIVIA

Who had a hit single with *Crocodile Rock* in 1972?

LETTER TRACKER

Begin in the central shaded square and follow a continuous path which will track from square to square, up, down and sideways, but never diagonally.

Your trail should cover every letter once only, in order to find:

Seventeen figures from classical mythology.

S	I	S	O	D	Y	S	S	E	U	S
E	M	D	N	A	P	S	E	L	L	I
N	E	O	R	N	V	V	A	A	C	H
E	U	S	A	R	U	R	E	N	I	M
T	S	A	P	U	L	C	A	N	R	A
I	D	G	E	T	M	E	D	A	T	C
D	I	S	S	A	E	O	U	R	L	E
O	O	U	E	Z	N	H	S	T	E	S
R	N	Y	S	X	I	P	A	E	M	I
H	S	U	U	S	N	E	P	T	U	N
P	A	E	H	T	E	M	O	R	P	E

SWEET BAD MUSIC

So who on earth was responsible for this lyric?

"But if this ever-changing world in which we live in …"

MISSING LETTERS

One letter of the alphabet is missing from each box. Find them all and place them in the order of the numbered boxes to reveal a six-letter word.

Word: _____

1	2	3
ATXON	YKAZS	WNXMV
HUWBP	BLRGT	AOSYG
ICVJQ	HQXCF	PBCHZ
ZRDFK	ODVMN	QKITF
LSYGE	PEWJU	ERJLU

4	5	6
AZRVG	AKSEZ	SXMTF
SLQFB	TFXYJ	LWGDC
JMECP	HBUMG	BHAJI
KUNXH	NCIRO	KYNUR
YTIWO	PWQVD	ZPOVQ

Answers to puzzles on the previous page

Dicey Arithmetic: The signs are x, ÷ and –.
Bermuda Triangle: UNDERESTIMATING
Proverbs and Sayings: People who live in glass houses should not throw stones.

143

BOX CLEVER

		&
↋	%	$
		⌣
		(

When the above is folded to form a cube, which one of the following can be produced?

A B C D E

WORDWHEEL

Using only the letters in the Wordwheel, you have ten minutes to find as many words as possible, none of which may be plurals, foreign words or proper nouns. Each word must be of three letters or more, all must contain the central letter and letters can only be used once in every word. There is at least one nine-letter word in the wheel.

Nine-letter word: _____

Wheel letters: I E S E R A B L M (centre M)

TOP TEN

SPAIN ☐
FRANCE ☐
HOLLAND ☐
ENGLAND ☐
ITALY ☐
GERMANY ☐
BELGIUM ☐
AUSTRIA ☐
SWITZERLAND ☐
PORTUGAL ☐

LAST MINUTE EXCUSES

In one minute, how many excuses can you find for:

Ignoring the mess

CHARACTER ASSIGNATION

Fill in the answers to the clues, across the grid. Then read down the diagonal line of seven squares, to reveal:
A mythological character.

1 Frenzied agitation
2 Cut of beef near the rump
3 Seventh color of the rainbow
4 Exonerating excuse
5 Explosive sound
6 And, also
7 Enclosed
8 Fifth letter of the alphabet

CHARACTER: _____

WHATEVER YOU DO, don't even THINK about...

Any of the following:

Having a sex-change

Root canal treatment

Having a prostate examination

SPELLING TEST

Which is the correctly spelled word?

MISCELLANEOUS ☐
MISELLANEOUS ☐
MISCELANEOUS ☐

BROKEN-HEARTED

Don't be halfhearted in your attempts to get these couples back together again! Match both sides of each heart, to reveal their names.

_____ & _____ _____ & _____ _____ & _____
_____ & _____ _____ & _____ _____ & _____

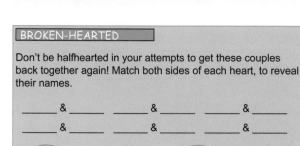

NIG HIL — A

IAN ILLA — B

ID MA — C

EL ARY — D

BREN IN — E

GE JAY — F

OFF NE — G

NOR ANT — H

ADR CAM — I

MAN HEA — J

DAV GEM — K

DAN GRID — L

EGG TIMER

Can you complete this puzzle in the time it takes to boil an egg? The answers to the clues are anagrams of the words immediately above and below, plus or minus a letter.

1 Tiny amount of liquid
2 Repeated
3 More senior
4 Traditional knowledge
5 Projecting bay window
6 Water heater
7 Draw into a situation

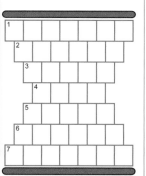

ODD ONE OUT

Which one is different to the rest?

A   B   C   D   E   F

Answers to puzzles on the previous page

Box Clever: B
Wordwheel: The nine-letter word is MISERABLE or MARBLEISE.
Character Assignation: 1 Hysteria, 2 Sirloin, 3 Violet, 4 Alibi, 5 Bang, 6 Too, 7 In, 8 E.
Character: Antigone.
Spelling Test: MISCELLANEOUS

ON THE TILES

In this puzzle, the eight tiles on the right must be fitted into the pattern in the middle so as to form four words reading across and five words reading down. No tile may be rotated!

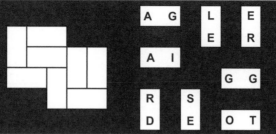

A	G
	L	E
	E	R
A	I
		G	G
R		S
D		E		O	T

LOOSE VOWELS

Someone has taken all the vowels out of what was once a completed crossword. Can you put them all back in again? You should use only those letters beneath the grid.

A A A A A
E E E E E E E E E E E
I I I I I
O O O O O
U U U U U

A MATCHING PAIR

Which are the only two that are identical in every way?

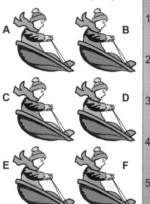

A B C D E F

Answers to puzzles on the previous page

Broken-hearted: A and D, E and L, F and G, H and J, I and B, K and C.
Egg Timer: 1 Droplet, 2 Retold, 3 Older, 4 Lore, 5 Oriel, 6 Boiler, 7 Embroil.
Odd One Out: B – The snowman's nose is back-to-front.

DESIGN YOUR OWN
PARTY DRESS

PAIR SHAPES

In the box below there are shapes in three different colors, red, white and blue. Any shape may have been rotated, but can you see which is the only shape to appear exactly twice in exactly the same color?

REAL WORDS

Which is the real word?

Pyknince ☐

Pachynsis ☐

Pyknint ☐

STARTER LETTER

Write down one each of the listed items, all of which must begin with the starter letter:

C

Country	
Tree	
Boy's name	
Girl's name	
River	
City	
Animal	
Make of car	
Drink	

CROSSED WORDS

Using only the letters above the diagram, fill in the squares to make a common two-word phrase, one word reading down and the other across.

A E E H I K L R W

PRE-FAME NAME GAME

By what name do we know this famous person?

Gordon Matthew Sumner

MOVIE QUOTES

We give you a line, you tell us who said it and the film:

"My mother thanks you. My father thanks you. My sister thanks you. And I thank you."

Answers to puzzles on the previous page

On the Tiles:

E	G	G		
R	A	I	L	S
A	G	R	E	E
		D	O	T

Loose Vowels:

M	K		C	U	E	D
C	A	L	I	C	O		E
	O	W		N	E	A	T
A	R	R	I	V	E	D		O
L	I	E		I		G	N	U
B		A	M	A	T	E	U	R
E	C	R	U		O			R
I			S	P	O	U	S	E
T	R	E	E		K		E

A Matching Pair: D and E

147

CODEWORD

This is a crossword puzzle in code. Every number represents a different letter of the alphabet and this number remains the same throughout the puzzle. Use the letters either side of the grid as well as the check-box below the grid to keep a track on your progress.

Left side labels: A B C D E F G H I J K L M

Right side labels: N O P Q R S T U V W X Y Z

21	2	6	16	19	17	7		11	2	12	17	26	5	24
5		12		22		11	25	5			18		8	
2	22	5	24	2		22		2	24	15	4	17	25	9
24		1		4	10	4	17	7			24		4	
9	2	7	14	22		12			2	26	5	24	7	
	6			4	12	12	5	26	2	12			17	
7	11	14	13	5				2		5	19	17	15	14
	4		17			22	2	20	17	22		16		5
23	5	22	7	4	26	17		5		7	22	2	4	12
	23		5			6	17	3		5		19		12
1	5	7	12	17	6	16		17	22	10	2	4	24	9

(A I L shown at positions in grid)

| 1 | 2 | 3 | 4 | 5 | 6 | 7 | 8 | 9 | 10 | 11 | 12 | 13 |
| | A | | I | | | | | | | | L | |

| 14 | 15 | 16 | 17 | 18 | 19 | 20 | 21 | 22 | 23 | 24 | 25 | 26 |
| | | | | | | | | | | | | |

BRIEF SURVIVAL GUIDE

FAMILY CHRISTMAS:

1 Start earlier on the sherry
2 Finish late with the whiskey
3 Stuff enough food into your mouth to avoid having to speak

A IS TO B

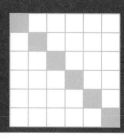

46 **2116**

A is to *B*

as *C* **63** is to

3969   **6939**

D   E

9369   **6993**

F   G

ARRANGING THINGS

If you fit six of these seven words into the grid, the word left over will appear reading down the shaded squares.

APOLLO DANUBE
GARAGE GAZEBO
GUZZLE MAGNUM
MODERN

Answers to puzzles on the previous page

Pair Shapes:
Real Words: Pachynsis
Crossed Words: Killer Whale
Pre-fame Name Game: Sting
Movie Quotes: George M Cohan (James Cagney) *Yankee Doodle Dandy* (1942)

EYE-SPY

I spy with my little eye something beginning with:

_____

MIRROR WRITING

Write this word upside down:

AMNESIA

_____

DO YOU KNOW...

...what happened on this date?

6 Sept 1620

WHAT DOES IT MEAN?

What is the meaning of the word

Inaniloquent

Answer: _____

COMPLETE THIS LIMERICK:

Miss Middleton had a great fright

Last evening, approaching midnight

She thought she saw bears

At the foot of her stairs

_____

SWEET BAD MUSIC

So who on earth was responsible for this lyric?

"Young, black and famous
With money hangin'
Out the anus"

DOMINADDITION

Can you place the remaining dominoes in their correct positions, so that the total number of spots in each of the four rows and five columns equals the sum at the end of that row or column?

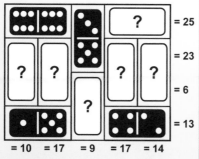

= 25
= 23
= 6
= 13

= 10 = 17 = 9 = 17 = 14

WHO AM I?

Old West action

I am:

_____

149

THE NAME GAME

Can you complete the six words reading across in such a way as to reveal the name of a well-known person in the shaded columns?

	R	I		E
	S	U		L
	U	S		I
	A	B		E
	I	D		D
	E	E		S

SHAPE RECOGNITION

Which are the only three pieces which will fit together to form a copy of this black shape?

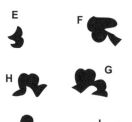

A   B

C   D

E   F

H   G

I   J

SECRET MISSION

Your secret mission (should you choose to accept it) is:

To look confused every time you are asked to do something.

REAL WORDS

Which is the real word?

Phrontistery ☐

Pecksnicious ☐

Pecksnipperty ☐

GET THE LOOK

Make the face:

CONCERNED

HEXAGONY

Can you place the hexagons in the grid, so that where any triangle touches another along a straight line, the contents of both are the same? One triangle is already filled.

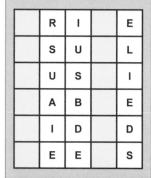

PRE-FAME NAME GAME

By what name do we know this famous person?

Virginia Katherine McMath

MUSIC TRIVIA

What is the common link between The Dave Clark 5, Fat Larry's Band and Harold Melvin and the Blue Notes?

Answers to puzzles on the previous page

Do You Know…: The *Mayflower* set sail with pilgrims, from Southampton, England.
What Does It Mean?: Pertaining to idle talk
Sweet Bad Music: Puff Daddy and Mase *Can't Nobody Hold Me Down*
Who Am I?: Clint Eastwood

Dominaddition:

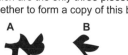

SNAKES AND LADDERS

This is a standard game, so when you land at the foot of a ladder, you climb it; and when you land on the head of a snake, you slide down its tail. You need to throw an exact number to land on 100 to win – counting backwards if you don't, eg if you land on 98 and throw a five, you will end up on 97. The dice is thrown for you and always lands in this recurring order: 1, 5, 6, 3, 2, 4, so you can start by immediately placing your counter on square 1. Good luck – hope you win!

100	99	98	97	96	95	94	93	92	91
81	82	83	84	85	86	87	88	89	90
80	79	78	77	76	75	74	73	72	71
61	62	63	64	65	66	67	68	69	70
60	59	58	57	56	55	54	53	52	51
41	42	43	44	45	46	47	48	49	50
40	39	38	37	36	35	34	33	32	31
21	22	23	24	25	26	27	28	29	30
20	19	18	17	16	15	14	13	12	11
1	2	3	4	5	6	7	8	9	10

TANGLED TACKLE

Which of these anglers has landed the fish?

A   B   C

PATCHWORK

Fit the letters A, B, C, D, E and F into the grid below, so that every horizontal row, every vertical column and every shape of six smaller squares contain six different letters. Some are already in place.

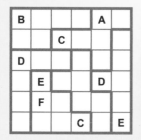

PRE-FAME NAME GAME

By what name do we know this famous person?

Roy Harold Scherer, Jr

WHERE ON H E A R T I ?

Where on Earth is Titless?

Answer: _____

QUOTE OF THE DAY

"Remember, today is the tomorrow you worried about yesterday."

Dale Carnegie

DICE-SECTION

Printed onto every one of the six numbered dice below are six letters (one per side), which can be rearranged to form the answer to each clue; however, some sides are invisible to you. Use the clues and write every answer into the grid. When correctly filled, the letters in the shaded squares, reading in the order 1 to 6, will spell the name of a Shakespearean heroine.

1 Native of Troy

2 Crush

3 American wild cat

4 Old English monetary unit

5 Skin disease

6 Pointless

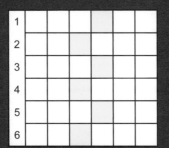

TOP TEN

INK

OIL PAINT

PENCIL

CHARCOAL

CRAYON

WATERCOLOR

CHALK

FELT-TIP PEN

ACRYLIC PAINT

SPRAY PAINT

ON TARGET

The answers to the clues read from the outer circle to the center, all ending with the same letter. When you've finished, the letters in the shaded ring will give a word.

1 Procreate, reproduce

2 Worn down, palled

3 Construct

4 Receded, flowed back

5 Vegetable food mixture

6 Change, improve

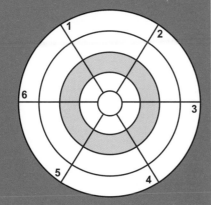

BRAINTEASER

What is the state capital of New York?

Answers to puzzles on the previous page

Tangled Tackle: Angler C
Pre-fame Name Game: Rock Hudson
Where on Earth?: Switzerland

Patchwork:

B	C	E	F	A	D
A	D	C	B	E	F
D	B	A	E	F	C
C	E	F	A	D	B
E	F	B	D	C	A
F	A	D	C	B	E

WHATEVER NEXT?

Which of the numbered alternatives comes next in this sequence:

| Y | N | T | H | O | ? |

| 1 A | 2 M |
| 3 Z | 4 B |

COUPLINGS

Apart from two, every word listed below can be coupled with one of the others to make another word or phrase. Rearrange the letters of the two which can't be paired together to form one word, the name of a large, voracious aquatic reptile.

1 SPIDER	2 BRUSH
3 MARE	4 COOL
5 CIDER	6 MONKEY
7 MONEY	8 PAINT
9 NIGHT	10 CLOTH
11 POCKET	12 GLIDER
13 HANG	14 TABLE

Answer: _____

WEATHER for PESSIMISTS

Today the weather will be:

Suspiciously calm and sunny

NAMED AND SHAMED

Self-important
_____

Selfish
_____

Self-centered

PICK 'N' MIX

Choose three words to describe your government:

Untrustworthy   Dictators
Trustworthy   Inept
Senseless   Liars
Inconsiderate   Lazy
Fascistic   Useless

UNLIKELY CANDIDATE

POPE

_____

JIGSAW CROSSWORD

Fit the blocks into the empty grid to form a complete crossword which, when finished, will be symmetrical, similar to the example seen here:

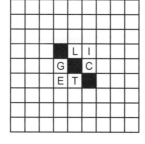

Answers to puzzles on the previous page

On Target: 1 Breed, 2 Jaded, 3 Build, 4 Ebbed, 5 Salad, 6 Amend.
The word is: EDIBLE
Brainteaser: Albany

Dice-Section:

T	R	O	J	A	N
S	Q	U	A	S	H
O	C	E	L	O	T
G	U	I	N	E	A
E	C	Z	E	M	A
F	U	T	I	L	E

TODAY'S GREATEST ACHIEVEMENT

Losing weight ☐

Gaining muscle ☐

Plucking eyebrows ☐

MASS HYSTERIAS

Today we are all going to:

Listen out for subliminal messages in everything we hear on the TV news.

THIS WEEK'S PHOBIAS

Thanatophobia – Morbid fear of death
Cibophobia – Fear of food
Heliophobia – Fear of the sun

BALANCING THE SCALES

Given that scales A and B balance perfectly, how many circles are needed to balance scale C?

WHO AM I?

He grew bogus

I am:

_____

WHATEVER YOU DO, don't even THINK about...

Any of the following:

Chemical toilets

Garbage dumps

Compost heaps

MY NEXT ARGUMENT

Who:
_____

Why:
_____

Where:
_____

PYRAMID PLUS

Every brick in this pyramid contains a number which is the sum of the two numbers below it, so that F=A+B, etc. No two bricks contain the same number, or just a zero, so work out the missing numbers!

O=133

M=   N=

J=   K=   L=38

F=   G=14   H=   I=17

A=5   B=   C=   D=   E=

STARTING LINE

Which three-letter word can be placed at the start, to form three seven-letter words?

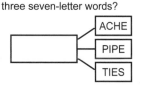

ACHE

PIPE

TIES

154

DIETING:
1 Put a lock on the fridge/ cupboards
2 Put a clothes peg on your nose to prevent any sense of smell and taste
3 Buy all your clothes two sizes too small

WAYS TO PASS THE TIME ...

Singing ☐

Making chutney ☐

Trying on clothes ☐

SUDOKU

The numbers from 1 to 9 inclusive need to be placed into the grid below in such a way that every horizontal row and vertical column contains nine different digits. In addition, each of the nine blocks of nine smaller squares should also contain nine different numbers. The clues are the numbers already placed.

	1		4					2
		4	1	9	3	5		
8		7	6			4		9
	2		5					3
4		9				2		1
7					1		6	
6		8			4	3		5
		1	3	2	7	8		
3					5		7	

WORDFILLER

Can you place all the listed words into the grid below?

3 letters
Add
Ant
Hat
Tan

4 letters
Gums
Last
Tare
Tuna

Undo
Used

5 letters
Adorn
Batch
Caste
Circa
Doric
Drain
Exact

Extra
Harsh
Lisle
Reins
Satyr
Sorry
Stoat
Tires
Vista

6 letters
Access
Heaven

7 letters
Backlog
Dietary

JOIN THE DOTS

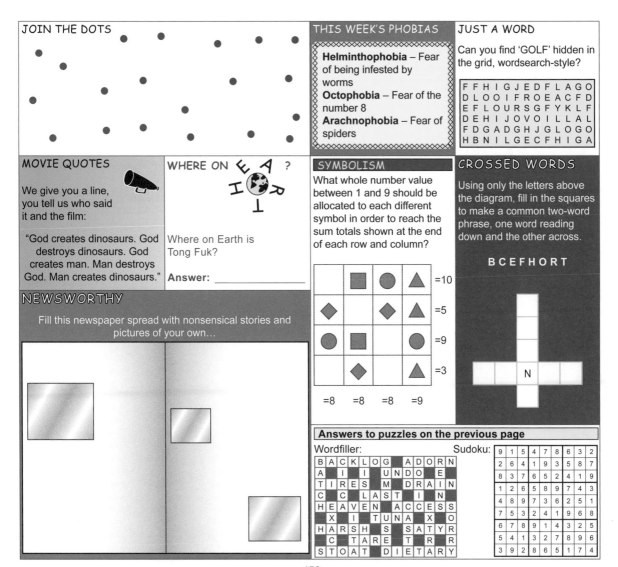

THIS WEEK'S PHOBIAS

Helminthophobia – Fear of being infested by worms

Octophobia – Fear of the number 8

Arachnophobia – Fear of spiders

JUST A WORD

Can you find 'GOLF' hidden in the grid, wordsearch-style?

```
F F H I G J E D F L A G O
D L O O I F R O E A C F D
E F L O U R S G F Y K L F
D E H I J O V O I L L A L
F D G A D G H J G L O G O
H B N I L G E C F H I G A
```

MOVIE QUOTES

We give you a line, you tell us who said it and the film:

"God creates dinosaurs. God destroys dinosaurs. God creates man. Man destroys God. Man creates dinosaurs."

WHERE ON EARTH?

Where on Earth is Tong Fuk?

Answer: _____

SYMBOLISM

What whole number value between 1 and 9 should be allocated to each different symbol in order to reach the sum totals shown at the end of each row and column?

	■	●	▲	=10
◆		◆	▲	=5
●	■		●	=9
	◆		▲	=3

=8 =8 =8 =9

CROSSED WORDS

Using only the letters above the diagram, fill in the squares to make a common two-word phrase, one word reading down and the other across.

B C E F H O R T

(crossword grid with N in centre)

NEWSWORTHY

Fill this newspaper spread with nonsensical stories and pictures of your own…

Answers to puzzles on the previous page

Wordfiller:

```
B A C K L O G   A D O R N
A   I   I   U N D O   E
T I R E S   M   D R A I N
C   C   L A S T   I   N
H E A V E N   A C C E S S
  X   I   T U N A   X   O
H A R S H   S   S A T Y R
  C   T A R E   T   R   R
S T O A T   D I E T A R Y
```

Sudoku:

9	1	5	4	7	8	6	3	2
2	6	4	1	9	3	5	8	7
8	3	7	6	5	2	4	1	9
1	2	6	5	8	9	7	4	3
4	8	9	7	3	6	2	5	1
7	5	3	2	4	1	9	6	8
6	7	8	9	1	4	3	2	5
5	4	1	3	2	7	8	9	6
3	9	2	8	6	5	1	7	4

ALL IN THE MIX

Rearrange each group of letters to reveal a type of plant; once they've been entered correctly, a tenth plant will be revealed in the shaded column.

1. Neck bar
2. Arrogant
3. Sinus scar
4. Rio dancer
5. The hare
6. Some title
7. Naïve orc
8. Owned bio
9. Verne, lad

BRAINTEASER

In which film did Marilyn Monroe play Sugar Kane?

TWO DOWN

Fit five of the seven listed words into the Across rows in the grid, so that the other two words read down the shaded columns numbered 2 and 3.

ABOUT   BERET
DEBIT   GRATE
PENNY   UNTIE
     UTTER

NUMB-SKULL

Fit the listed numbers into the grid, crossword-fashion.

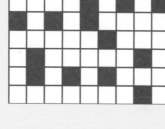

3 digits
255
263
521
538

4 digits
2198
3200
3455
4353
4433
4542
5868
6995
7304
7834
8033
9480

5 digits
12484
15327
32578
33080
38736
45425
68243
71353

7 digits
5089515
7841903

MUSIC TRIVIA

Which band had hits with *Linger* and *Dreams*?

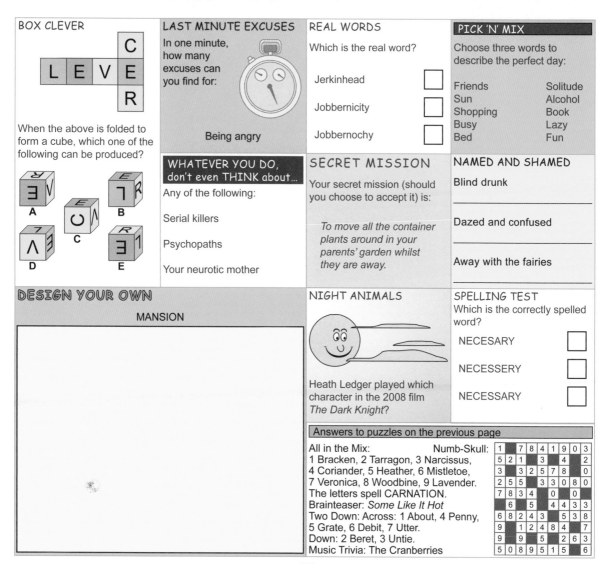

BOX CLEVER

When the above is folded to form a cube, which one of the following can be produced?

A B C D E

LAST MINUTE EXCUSES

In one minute, how many excuses can you find for:

Being angry

WHATEVER YOU DO, don't even THINK about...

Any of the following:

Serial killers

Psychopaths

Your neurotic mother

REAL WORDS

Which is the real word?

Jerkinhead ☐

Jobbernicity ☐

Jobbernochy ☐

SECRET MISSION

Your secret mission (should you choose to accept it) is:

To move all the container plants around in your parents' garden whilst they are away.

PICK 'N' MIX

Choose three words to describe the perfect day:

Friends	Solitude
Sun	Alcohol
Shopping	Book
Busy	Lazy
Bed	Fun

NAMED AND SHAMED

Blind drunk

_____

Dazed and confused

_____

Away with the fairies

_____

DESIGN YOUR OWN

MANSION

NIGHT ANIMALS

Heath Ledger played which character in the 2008 film *The Dark Knight*?

SPELLING TEST

Which is the correctly spelled word?

NECESARY ☐

NECESSERY ☐

NECESSARY ☐

KEYWORD

Simply fill in the letters missing from the different words numbered 1-6 and enter them into the numbered boxes, to reveal the hidden keyword. Take care, however, as some may have more than one possible letter which could fit: for example S — M E might be either SAME or SOME.

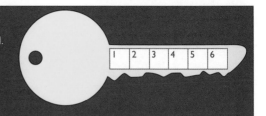

| 1 | 2 | 3 | 4 | 5 | 6 |

1 SOL—ER
2 PA—RED
3 PRE—ENT
4 SWA—PING
5 CL—AVE
6 YEAR—ING

WORDSEARCH

Can you find all of the listed musical instruments in the grid? Words may run in either a forwards or backwards direction, horizontally, vertically or diagonally, but always in a straight, uninterrupted line.

BANJO
BELL
BUGLE
CELLO
CORNET
FIFE
GONG
HARP
LUTE
LYRE
MOOG

```
C M D G H L N S B G O K E
T O W A V E D A O V U D F
M I R R S M T O G W A N I
P P M N U X M M C R L B F
J C M P E U J G H H O V H
E E B W A T O R E P I P Y
T L N Q A N E L Y A V N T
E E G K G H I D R V C O V
R L W U T A S E T I L Z R
Y U T I B R B D O O F X B
L K Z U J E O T C L L K A
R U T A C L T C C I B S N
Y I T V L S I S T N U E J
O L L E C P A R A S Z Y O
Z N B E L T S I H W N I T
```

ORGAN   SHAWM   UKULELE
PICCOLO   TIMPANI   VIOLA
PIPE   TIN WHISTLE   VIOLIN
REBEC   TUBA   ZITHER

TOP FIVE

Best songs for a funeral:

1 _____

_____

2 _____

_____

3 _____

_____

4 _____

_____

5 _____

_____

SWEET BAD MUSIC

So who on earth was responsible for this lyric?

"I don't like cities
But I like New York
Other places
Make me feel like a dork"

Answers to puzzles on the previous page

Box Clever: E
Real Words: Jerkinhead
Night Animals: The Joker
Spelling Test: NECESSARY

SIMPLE AS A,B,C

In the grid, each row across, column down and diagonal line of six squares should contain two each of A, B and C. The clues relate to the squares only in that row or column. We give as many clues as we think you need (including any letters already in the grid), so can you place the letters correctly?

Across:
1 The Cs are between the As.
2 The As are further right than the Cs.
3 The As are further left than the Cs.
4 The Bs are further right than the Cs.
6 The Bs are further right than the Cs.

Down:
4 The As are higher than the Cs.
5 The As are lower than the Cs.
6 The Cs are between the As.

	1	2	3	4	5	6
1						
2						
3						
4						
5						
6						

WORD LADDER

Change one letter at a time (but not the position of any letter) to make a new word – and move from the word at the top of the ladder to the word at the bottom using the exact number of rungs provided.

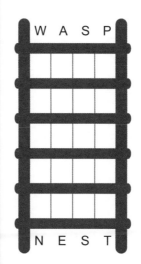

W A S P

N E S T

GOOD IMPRESSIONS

Can you pair up these door keys with the impressions of their ends?

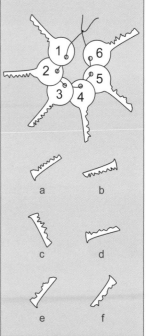

a   b

c   d

e   f

PRE-FAME NAME GAME

By what name do we know this famous person?

Lily Chauchoin

ALL AT SEA

Sir Francis Drake set off to circumnavigate the globe in 1577 in the *Pelican*, but renamed the ship half way through his voyage. What new name did he give it?

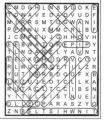

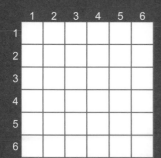

LEADING LADIES

Which of these women is walking the dog?

A

B

C

DO YOU KNOW...

...what happened on this date?

21 August 1959

WHAT DOES IT MEAN?

What is the meaning of the word

Nihilarian

Answer: _____

_____

WHAT'S IN A NAME?

How many words (other names included) can you make from the name:

BARTHOLOMEW

_____

_____

_____

_____

SUM THOUGHTS

What is the sum total of all of the following two-digit numbers?

26

44

87

40

17

63   48

USE YOUR IMAGINATION

Can you fill each of these boxes with a different make of car?

WEATHER for OPTIMISTS

Today the weather will be:

Misty with drizzle like a delicious facial spritz.

Answers to puzzles on the previous page

Word Ladder – One solution is:
WASP, wash, mash, mesh, mess, ness, NEST.
Good Impressions: 1-d, 2-a, 3-b, 4-f, 5-e, 6-c.
Pre-fame Name Game:
Claudette Colbert
All at Sea: *The Golden Hind*

Simple as A,B,C:

B	A	C	B	C	A
C	C	A	A	B	B
A	B	B	A	C	C
A	A	C	C	B	B
B	B	A	C	A	C
C	C	B	B	A	A

ON THE TILES

In this puzzle, the eight tiles on the right must be fitted into the pattern in the middle so as to form four words reading across and five words reading down. No tile may be rotated!

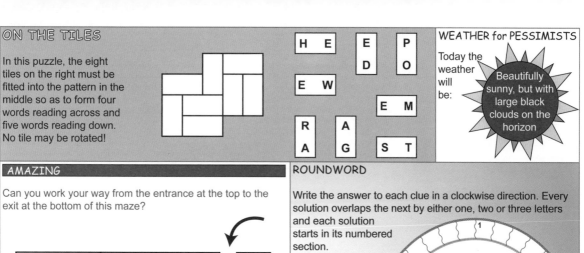

H	E		E		P
E			D		O
E	W				
				E	M
R		A			
A		G		S	T

AMAZING

Can you work your way from the entrance at the top to the exit at the bottom of this maze?

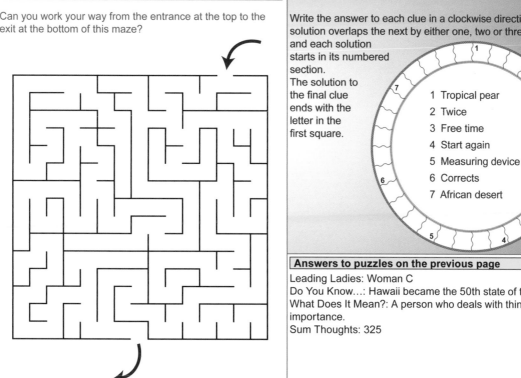

ROUNDWORD

Write the answer to each clue in a clockwise direction. Every solution overlaps the next by either one, two or three letters and each solution starts in its numbered section. The solution to the final clue ends with the letter in the first square.

1 Tropical pear
2 Twice
3 Free time
4 Start again
5 Measuring device
6 Corrects
7 African desert

Answers to puzzles on the previous page

Leading Ladies: Woman C
Do You Know…: Hawaii became the 50th state of the USA.
What Does It Mean?: A person who deals with things lacking importance.
Sum Thoughts: 325

PARTNERS IN RHYME

Each of the pairs below is a rhyme for a familiar phrase. Can you identify them?

1. Thin and conic _____

2. Snide and rested _____

3. Brat and louse _____

4. Slack and tight _____

STARTING LINE

Which three-letter word can be placed at the start, to form three seven-letter words?

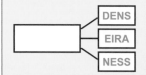

MUSIC TRIVIA

In music, which band consists of Billy Gibbons, Dusty Hill and Frank Beard?

GET THE LOOK

Make the face:

SEXY

IN CHAINS

This chain of letters contains the names of three birds. The letters are in the correct order but need to be picked out.

T F U I D N R O K D E C Y O H

_____   _____

_____

CROSSWISE

Rearrange the six scrambled groups of letters to form words and then decide where each fits in the grid. Some letters are already in place.

AAABRZ	ACERSS
AFHLSY	ALOPRT
CEEPRY	EEEFRZ

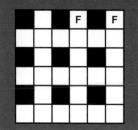

WHOLESOME FUN

In this puzzle, you need to find a five-letter word by deciding which common letter has been removed from the trios of words on each line.
Enter that letter into the circle at the end of each row and the word will be revealed reading downwards.

_RAB	PA_K	A_RE
F_OG	G_ID	A_CH
G_AL	L_UT	JUD_
A_IA	_AGA	AXI_
VA_T	I_LE	_AIL

LAST MINUTE EXCUSES

In one minute, how many excuses can you find for:

Unkempt hair

TOP TEN

SHOUT ☐
SING ☐
TALK ☐
LAUGH ☐
YELL ☐
WHISPER ☐
YODEL ☐
CRY ☐
RECITE ☐
SIGH ☐

SPOT THE SAME

Only two of these modern abstract paintings are identical in every way: which?

THE NAME GAME

Can you complete the six words reading across in such a way as to reveal the name of a well-known person in the shaded columns?

	O	R		E
	E	A		M
	N	G		R
	O	V		R
	T	O		E
	O	N		Y

NUMBER BOX

In this puzzle, simply use the hints given to enter nine different numbers 1-9 in their correct boxes.

4 is directly below 1
2 is two squares below 6
9 is two squares right of 1
7 is two squares below 3
8 is two squares left of 6

NIGHT ANIMALS

Native to Madagascar, which nocturnal primate has a bony elongated finger that it uses to tap on trees to find its food?

ON TARGET

The answers to the clues read from the outer circle to the center, all ending with the same letter. When you've finished, the letters in the shaded ring will give a word.

1 Stony
2 God
3 High-spirited
4 Rot away
5 Showy, loud
6 Awful, disgusting

TOP FIVE

Best songs for working to:

1 _____
2 _____
3 _____
4 _____
5 _____

CELEBRITY WRESTLING

TOM CRUISE

-v-

POPE BENEDICT XVI

UNFINISHED PICTURE

Can you complete this doodle?

QUOTE OF THE DAY

"I can resist everything except temptation."

Oscar Wilde

UNLIKELY CANDIDATE

MAKE-UP ARTIST

DO YOU KNOW...

...what happened in the Far East on this date?

1 July 1997

JIGSAW CROSSWORD

Fit the blocks into the empty grid to form a complete crossword which, when finished, will be symmetrical, similar to the example seen here:

NAMED AND SHAMED

Worst friend

_____

Worst lover

_____

Worst family member

_____

MOVIE QUOTES

We give you a line, you tell us who said it and the film:

"You can't handle the truth!"

WHERE ON 𝐇𝐄𝐀𝐑𝐓𝐇 ?

Where on Earth is Wank?

Answer: _____

TODAY'S GREATEST ACHIEVEMENT

Walking ☐

Running ☐

Wandering ☐

IN SHAPE

How many rectangles can you see here?

GET THE LOOK

Make the face:

CRAVING

DOMINOLOGICAL

What is the value of the question mark?

?

PYRAMID PLUS

Every brick in this pyramid contains a number which is the sum of the two numbers below it, so that F=A+B, etc. No two bricks contain the same number, or just a zero, so work out the missing numbers!

O=110

M=   N=

J=37   K=   L=

F=21   G=   H=11   I=

A=   B=   C=   D=7   E=

WHO AM I?

He's jail cock man

I am:

_____

BRAINTEASER

Which planet in the solar system is named after the Roman messenger to the Gods?

WAYS TO PASS THE TIME ...

Sorting socks ☐

Flying ☐

Sleeping ☐

THIS WEEK'S PHOBIAS

Chromophobia – Fear of colors
Dendrophobia – Fear of trees
Ephebiphobia – Fear of teenagers

LETTER TRACKER

Begin in the central shaded square and follow a continuous path which will track from square to square, up, down and sideways, but never diagonally.

Your trail should cover every letter once only, in order to find:

Sixteen girls' names.

N	C	A	I	N	E	C	A	R	L	A
E	H	M	A	R	D	E	V	V	E	N
E	A	R	B	A	N	C	E	I	G	E
R	U	R	A	S	S	A	T	A	Y	N
M	A	B	R	E	N	M	S	L	K	A
E	L	A	U	A	L	E	Y	R	A	F
C	O	R	A	M	A	L	A	H	T	F
I	E	C	T	A	R	G	N	C	H	I
N	S	I	R	E	B	A	I	E	E	T
Y	H	I	I	N	E	R	E	T	R	E
E	L	R	H	P	E	S	O	J	I	N

SUM TOTAL

Place the digits 1-9, one per square, so that the sums are correct, according to the totals at the ends of the rows and columns. The calculations should be done in the order in which they appear, for example 6–2x5=20 should be read as 6–2(=4), then 4x5=20.

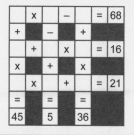

SECRET MISSION

Your secret mission (should you choose to accept it) is:

To say "Whatever" every time someone asks you any question.

BRIEF SURVIVAL GUIDE

JOB INTERVIEW:
1 Rehearse over-eager workaholic persona the night before
2 Try to remember what the job description is
3 Wash and dress before going

Answers to puzzles on the previous page

Movie Quotes: Col Nathan Jessup (Jack Nicholson) *A Few Good Men* (1992)
Where on Earth?: Germany   In Shape: 18.
Dominological: 5 at the top and 6 at the bottom; the top number increases by 1, then 2, then 1, and the bottom number increases by 2, then 1, then 2.
Pyramid Plus: A=9, B=12, C=4, D=7, E=1, F=21, G=16, H=11, I=8, J=37, K=27, L=19, M=64, N=46, O=110.
Who Am I?: Michael Jackson

ELIMINATION

Every oval shape contains a different letter from A to K inclusive. Use the clues to determine their locations. Reference in the clues to 'due' means in any location along the same horizontal or vertical line.

1 I is due south of A, which is next to and due east of K.

2 I is due east of C, which is next to and due south of J.

3 G is due south of B, which is due west of H, which is further north than C.

4 D is further north than F, further west than C and further south than E.

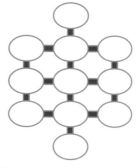

TWO-WORD HOROSCOPES

Aries – not this

Taurus – clinically insane

Gemini – big man

Cancer – hospital food

Leo – break out

Virgo – best times

Libra – you know...

Scorpio – dark thoughts

Sagittarius – jolly good

Capricorn – don't forget

Aquarius – tediously dull

Pisces – hard work

DESIGN YOUR OWN

SWIMMING POOL

MY NEXT MISTAKE

What:

_____

Where:

_____

Why:

_____

Answers to puzzles on the previous page

What Does It Mean?: A dumpster diver; one who extracts valuable things from trash.
Brainteaser: Mercury
Letter Tracker: Lauren, Melanie, Chrystal, Katherine, Tiffany, Genevieve, Cassandra, Barbara, Margaret, Josephine, Beatrice, Shirley, Nicole, Maureen, Charmaine, Carla.

Sum Total:

8	x	9	–	4
+		–		+
1	+	7	x	2
x		+		x
5	x	3	+	6

TOTAL CONCENTRATION

Can you fill in the missing numbers so that each row, each column and two longest diagonal lines meet the totals given?

							62
4	17	10	6		7	3	65
18		7	13		11	14	82
	20		9	16	1		74
17	4			11	14	5	72
	13	9	18	12		6	94
2	12	10		15		1	80
5		20		12	3	8	73
73	95	73	79	92	72	56	63

WORD LADDER

Change one letter at a time (but not the position of any letter) to make a new word – and move from the word at the top of the ladder to the word at the bottom using the exact number of rungs provided.

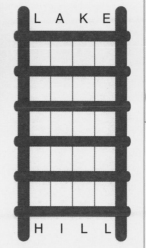

STARTING LINE

Which three-letter word can be placed at the start, to form three seven-letter words?

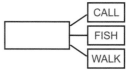

WEATHER for OPTIMISTS

Today the weather will be:

Hot and humid, like a sauna detox.

TIED UP AT PRESENT

Which boy is holding the string attached to the present?

TWO DOWN

Fit five of the seven listed words into the Across rows in the grid, so that the other two words read down the shaded columns numbered 2 and 3.

ATLAS   CLIFF
DEFER   LATER
PANDA   STREW
USURY

1	2		3	
4				
5				
6				
7				

PICK 'N' MIX

Choose three words to describe your favorite movie:

Bloodthirsty	Evil
Psychological	Death
Music	Scary
Slasher	Brutal
Suspense	Comedy

Answers to puzzles on the previous page

Elimination:

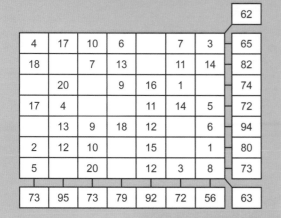

169

CLOCKWORDS

It's a race against the clock…
How many common words of three or more different letters can you make from those on the clock face (without using plurals, proper nouns or abbreviations) in ten minutes? All words must contain BOTH the letters indicated by the hands on the clock.

QUOTE OF THE DAY

"Show me a sane man and I will cure him for you. "
Carl Gustav Jung

WEATHER for PESSIMISTS

Today the weather will be:

Windy: a hurricane will flatten your house

DICEY ARITHMETIC

Using three of the arithmetical signs ÷, −, x and +, can you achieve the correct total?

    =

BERMUDA TRIANGLE

Travel through the 'Bermuda Triangle' by visiting one room at a time and collecting a letter from each. You can enter the outside passageway as often as you like, but can only visit each room once. When you've completed your tour, the 15 letters spell out a word.

PROVERBS AND SAYINGS

The letters on the tiles were once all in place, but dropped out, falling in a straight line into the lower grid. Some tiles dropped earlier than others, so those on the lowest row aren't all from the same row in the grid above. Can you put them back into position in order to reveal a well-known proverb or saying?

D	A			E								
H	F	M	'	I			I	C	C	E		A
H	I	N	A	T	R	F	U	I	S	H		D	,
I	O	T	M	T	T	S	W	R	T	T	E	Y	O	U

JOIN THE DOTS

Answers to puzzles on the previous page

Total Concentration: From left to right, top to bottom the missing numbers are: 18, 11, 8, 7, 2, 19, 15, 6, 20, 16, 20, 20, 18 and 7.
Word Ladder – One solution is: One solution is LAKE, lane, line, lint, lilt, hilt, HILL.
Starting Line: CAT
Tied up at Present: Boy A
Two Down: Across: 1 Panda, 4 Strew, 5 Cliff, 6 Later, 7 Usury. Down: 2 Atlas, 3 Defer.

MISSING LINKS

Which word links the one on the left with the one on the right? We've done the first one, and when you've finished them all, the first letters of the link words will spell another word.

BLACK	**MAIL**	BOX
BLACK		PICK
EVER		PEPPER
CONCERT		MARK
PART		BOMB

LETTER TRACKER

Begin in the central shaded square and follow a continuous path which will track from square to square, up, down and sideways, but never diagonally.

Your trail should cover every letter once only, in order to find:

Sixteen boys' names.

N	I	E	F	E	N	K	E	E	R	W
A	D	R	H	T	N	E	C	N	L	A
N	D	O	J	N	E	H	P	E	M	A
T	S	S	E	P	H	S	T	T	L	I
E	W	U	O	R	F	I	O	S	L	I
R	A	G	D	E	G	R	P	R	S	W
T	T	L	K	D	R	H	H	E	U	I
I	R	A	C	E	E	C	Y	N	E	L
S	T	S	I	R	G	O	R	R	O	C
N	A	N	E	V	I	E	N	H	O	S
D	A	V	I	D	L	L	I	C	L	A

THE NAME GAME

Can you complete the six words reading across in such a way as to reveal the name of a well-known person in the shaded columns?

	R	A		E
	S	H		R
	A	L		D
	R	I		E
	T	H		S
	O	U		D

MISSING LETTERS

One letter of the alphabet is missing from each box. Find them all and place them in the order of the numbered boxes to reveal a six-letter word.

Word: _____

1	2	3
NMUXA	LSQFA	NYHIG
OKJQB	YOXBJ	PTSLC
ISGVC	IGMHD	KXFDE
HDYZF	ZUTNK	QAUWO
EWPTL	CVWRP	MVRBZ

4	5	6
DRTOL	WOLPM	UQHPG
VCXKH	ZRYQJ	FILAE
BWMJZ	DHKGB	YNRBC
GPQAY	USTNF	VODJS
NUSFI	VIXEA	WZXKM

Answers to puzzles on the previous page

Dicey Arithmetic: The signs are +, x and –.
Bermuda Triangle: CONDESCENDINGLY
Proverbs and Sayings: If at first you don't succeed, hit it with a hammer.

BOX CLEVER

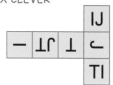

When the above is folded to form a cube, which one of the following can be produced?

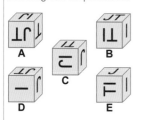

A B C D E

WORDWHEEL

Using only the letters in the Wordwheel, you have ten minutes to find as many words as possible, none of which may be plurals, foreign words or proper nouns. Each word must be of three letters or more, all must contain the central letter and letters can only be used once in every word. There is at least one nine-letter word in the wheel.

Nine-letter word: _____

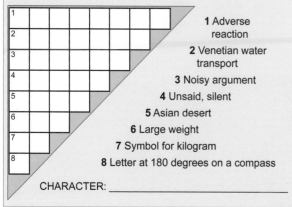

ODD ONE OUT

Which of these letters is the odd one out, and why?

A E F H

I K L M

N P T V

W X Y Z

LAST MINUTE EXCUSES

In one minute, how many excuses can you find for:

Not making the bed

MUSIC TRIVIA

In 1987, who had a hit with *La Bamba*?

CHARACTER ASSIGNATION

Fill in the answers to the clues, across the grid. Then read down the diagonal line of seven squares, to reveal:
A character created by Agatha Christie.

1 Adverse reaction
2 Venetian water transport
3 Noisy argument
4 Unsaid, silent
5 Asian desert
6 Large weight
7 Symbol for kilogram
8 Letter at 180 degrees on a compass

CHARACTER: _____

GET THE LOOK

Make the face:

HOPELESS

SPELLING TEST

Which is the correctly spelled word?

FLORESCENT ☐

FLUORESCENT ☐

FLUORECENT ☐

BROKEN-HEARTED

Don't be halfhearted in your attempts to get these couples back together again! Match both sides of each heart, to reveal their names.

_____ & _____   _____ & _____   _____ & _____

_____ & _____   _____ & _____   _____ & _____

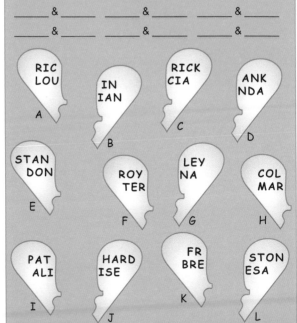

A — RIC LOU

B — IN IAN

C — RICK CIA

D — ANK NDA

E — STAN DON

F — ROY TER

G — LEY NA

H — COL MAR

I — PAT ALI

J — HARD ISE

K — FR BRE

L — STON ESA

EGG TIMER

Can you complete this puzzle in the time it takes to boil an egg? The answers to the clues are anagrams of the words immediately above and below, plus or minus a letter.

1 Belief that there is no God
2 British river
3 Water vapor
4 Domesticate
5 Chemical element such as iron, lead, etc
6 Regret strongly
7 Softly bright or radiant

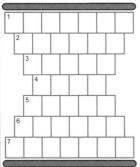

ODD ONE OUT

Which one is different to the rest?

A	B
CHAIR	COW

C	D
BOOK	DOG

E	F
FROG	TABLE

Answers to puzzles on the previous page

Box Clever: A
Wordwheel: The nine-letter word is RESONANCE.
Odd One Out: P, the other letters are all made up of straight lines, but P is made of a curve and a straight line.
Music Trivia: Los Lobos
Character Assignation: 1 Backlash, 2 Gondola, 3 Fracas, 4 Tacit, 5 Gobi, 6 Ton, 7 Kg, 8 S.
Character: Hastings.
Spelling Test: FLUORESCENT

ON THE TILES

In this puzzle, the eight tiles on the right must be fitted into the pattern in the middle so as to form four words reading across and five words reading down. No tile may be rotated!

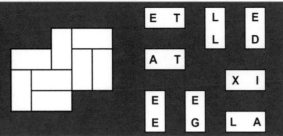

LOOSE VOWELS

Someone has taken all the vowels out of what was once a completed crossword. Can you put them all back in again? You should use only those letters beneath the grid.

A A A A A A A

E E E E E E E E E

I I

O O O O O O

U U U U

A MATCHING PAIR

Which are the only two that are identical in every way?

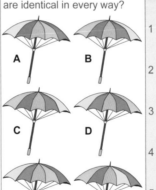

Answers to puzzles on the previous page

Broken-hearted: A and J, E and G, F and L, H and B, I and C, K and D.

Egg Timer: 1 Atheism, 2 Thames, 3 Steam, 4 Tame, 5 Metal, 6 Lament, 7 Lambent.

Odd One Out: C – All of the others have legs.

DESIGN YOUR OWN
SPEEDBOAT

PAIR SHAPES

In the box below there are shapes in three different colors, red, white and blue. Any shape may have been rotated, but can you see which is the only shape to appear exactly twice in exactly the same color?

REAL WORDS

Which is the real word?

Amphigory ☐

Absocelleny ☐

Absodoculane ☐

STARTER LETTER

Write down one each of the listed items, all of which must begin with the starter letter:

M

Country	
Tree	
Boy's name	
Girl's name	
River	
City	
Animal	
Make of car	
Drink	

CROSSED WORDS

Using only the letters above the diagram, fill in the squares to make a common two-word phrase, one word reading down and the other across.

A E F H I R S T T

PRE-FAME NAME GAME

By what name do we know this famous person?

Mary Frances Reynolds

WHAT DOES IT MEAN?

What is the meaning of the word

Limerence

Answer: _____

_____

175

CODEWORD

This is a crossword puzzle in code. Every number represents a different letter of the alphabet and this number remains the same throughout the puzzle. Use the letters either side of the grid as well as the check-box below the grid to keep a track on your progress.

A | 8 | 7 | 2 **N** | 20 **I** | 26 **B** | 24 | 10 | ■ | 10 | 12 | 24 | 13 | 23 | 21 | 17 | N
B | 13 | ■ | 13 | ■ | 13 | ■ | 13 | 10 | 11 | ■ | ■ | 3 | ■ | 9 | ■ | O
C | 10 | 21 | 5 | 21 | 23 | ■ | 15 | ■ | 23 | 21 | 25 | 8 | 20 | 18 | 21 | P
D | 20 | ■ | 13 | ■ | 23 | 21 | 13 | 17 | 1 | ■ | ■ | 2 | ■ | 6 | ■ | Q
E | 10 | 13 | 6 | 5 | 8 | ■ | 23 | ■ | ■ | ■ | 26 | 1 | 22 | 13 | 1 | R
F | ■ | 26 | ■ | ■ | 22 | 23 | 20 | 3 | 3 | 6 | 21 | ■ | ■ | 20 | ■ | S
G | 17 | 8 | 4 | 21 | 10 | ■ | ■ | ■ | 13 | ■ | 16 | 21 | 23 | 7 | 10 | T
H | ■ | 6 | ■ | 23 | ■ | ■ | 13 | 6 | 6 | 8 | 22 | ■ | 13 | ■ | 14 | U
I | 16 | 20 | 16 | 13 | 2 | 20 | 18 | ■ | 13 | ■ | 21 | 7 | 26 | 21 | 23 | V
J | ■ | 10 | ■ | 10 | ■ | 14 | 21 | 9 | ■ | 21 | ■ | 26 | ■ | 24 | ■ | W
K | 22 | 14 | 21 | 21 | 17 | 6 | 21 | ■ | 1 | 13 | 2 | 19 | 20 | 2 | 3 | X
(Y / Z labels continue on right)

1	2	3	4	5	6	7	8	9	10	11	12	13
	N											

14	15	16	17	18	19	20	21	22	23	24	25	26
						I						B

ARRANGING THINGS

If you fit six of these seven words into the grid, the word left over will appear reading down the shaded squares.

BADGER BOFFIN
FORGET FROZEN
MARGIN MEMORY
SINGLE

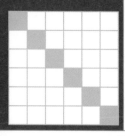

A IS TO B

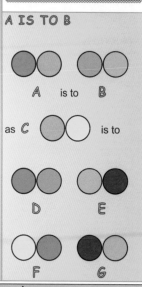

A is to B as C ◯◯ is to

D   E
F   G

EYE-SPY

I spy with my little eye something beginning with:

S

_____

MIRROR WRITING

Write this word upside down:

FAMILY

_____

DO YOU KNOW...

...what happened in the North Atlantic on this date?

31 October 1941

PRE-FAME NAME GAME

By what name do we know this famous person?

Sophia Scicoloni

COMPLETE THIS LIMERICK:

There was a young man from Devizes

Whose teeth were all different sizes

When he bit into bread

And chewed, people said

_____

SWEET BAD MUSIC

So who on earth was responsible for this lyric?

"War is stupid
And people are stupid"

DOMINADDITION

Can you place the remaining dominoes in their correct positions, so that the total number of spots in each of the four rows and five columns equals the sum at the end of that row or column?

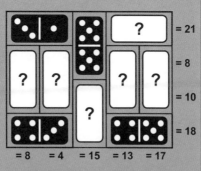

= 21
= 8
= 10
= 18

= 8   = 4   = 15   = 13   = 17

WHO AM I?

Best PR in years

I am:

_____

Answers to puzzles on the previous page

A is to B: E – They are pairs of rainbow colors, with the intervening color omitted.

Arranging Things:
Across (from the top): Memory, Badger, Forget, Single, Boffin, Frozen.
Down: Margin.

Codeword:

O	M	N	I	B	U	S		S	Q	U	A	R	E	D
A		A		A		A	S	P		G		X		
S	E	V	E	R		F		R	E	J	O	I	C	E
I		A		R	E	A	D	Y		N		L		
S	A	L	V	O		R			B	Y	W	A	Y	
	B			W	R	I	G	G	L	E			I	
D	O	Z	E	S			A		T	E	R	M	S	
	L		R		A	L	L	O	W		A		H	
T	I	T	A	N	I	C		A		E	M	B	E	R
	S		S		H	E	X		E		B		U	
W	H	E	E	D	L	E		Y	A	N	K	I	N	G

177

TWO-WORD HOROSCOPES

Aries – go now!

Taurus – glad tidings

Gemini – bossy boots

Cancer – last chance

Leo – big head

Virgo – sweet dreams

Libra – dirty money

Scorpio – useless ideas

Sagittarius – big win

Capricorn – love yourself

Aquarius – start talking

Pisces – tough love

SHAPE RECOGNITION

Which are the only three pieces which will fit together to form a copy of this black shape?

A   B   C   D

E   F

H   G

I   J

REAL WORDS

Which is the real word?

Rhadamanthine

Rhapsononite

Rhapsodobitulist

SECRET MISSION

Your secret mission (should you choose to accept it) is:

Too dangerous to even speak about. Say nothing.

ALL AT SEA

What was the name of Han Solo's ship in *Star Wars*?

HEXAGONY

Can you place the hexagons in the grid, so that where any triangle touches another along a straight line, the contents of both are the same? One triangle is already filled.

PRE-FAME NAME GAME

By what name do we know this famous person?

Norma Egstrom

_____

MUSIC TRIVIA

Which well-known band was formed in 1973 by brothers Angus and Malcolm Young?

Answers to puzzles on the previous page

Do You Know…: The American destroyer *Reuben James* sank after being torpedoed by a German U-boat.
Pre-fame Name Game: Sophia Loren
Sweet Bad Music: Culture Club
The War Song
Who Am I?: Britney Spears

Dominaddition:

3	1	5	6	6
0	0	5	1	2
1	0	3	2	4
4	3	2	4	5

SNAKES AND LADDERS

This is a standard game, so when you land at the foot of a ladder, you climb it; and when you land on the head of a snake, you slide down its tail. You need to throw an exact number to land on 100 to win – counting backwards if you don't, eg if you land on 98 and throw a five, you will end up on 97. The dice is thrown for you and always lands in this recurring order: 4, 3, 2, 1, 6, 5, so you can start by immediately placing your counter on square 4. Good luck – hope you win!

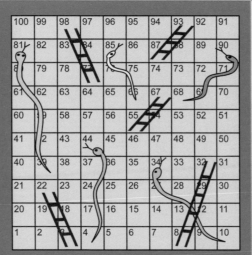

TANGLED TACKLE

Which of these anglers has landed the fish?

A   B   C

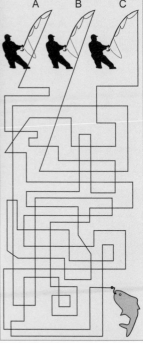

PATCHWORK

Fit the letters A, B, C, D, E and F into the grid below, so that every horizontal row, every vertical column and every shape of six smaller squares contain six different letters. Some are already in place.

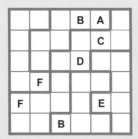

MOVIE QUOTES

We give you a line, you tell us who said it and the film:

"You talkin' to me?"

WHERE ON EARTH?

Where on Earth is Iron Knob?

Answer: _____

QUOTE OF THE DAY

"As to marriage or celibacy, let a man take the course he will. He will be sure to repent."

Socrates

Answers to puzzles on the previous page

Shape Recognition:
B, E and J
Real Words: Rhadamanthine
All at Sea: *The Millennium Falcon*
Pre-fame Name Game: Peggy Lee
Music Trivia: AC/DC

Hexagony:

DICE-SECTION

Printed onto every one of the six numbered dice below are six letters (one per side), which can be rearranged to form the answer to each clue; however, some sides are invisible to you. Use the clues and write every answer into the grid. When correctly filled, the letters in the shaded squares, reading in the order 1 to 6, will spell out a metallic element.

1 Sign of the zodiac

2 Widely-used internet search engine

3 Egyptian god of tombs and the underworld

4 Early form of mathematical calculator

5 Maker of garments

6 Form of written communication

Dice 1: R, A, N
Dice 2: L, E, G
Dice 3: S, I, N
Dice 4: S, U, B
Dice 5: O, A, R
Dice 6: E, E, L

PARTNERS IN RHYME

Each of the pairs below is a rhyme for a familiar phrase. Can you identify them?

1. Tart and droll

_____

2. Leer and swear

_____

3. Scarred and passed

_____

4. Mutts and colts

_____

ON TARGET

The answers to the clues read from the outer circle to the center, all ending with the same letter. When you've finished, the letters in the shaded ring will give a word.

1 Aviator

2 Force out, eg eject from a property

3 Religious dogma

4 Group of eight

5 Expert, skillful

6 Divide, cleave

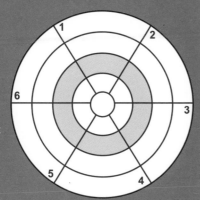

BRAINTEASER

Which famous person was assassinated by John Wilkes Booth?

Answers to puzzles on the previous page

Tangled Tackle: Angler B
Movie Quotes: Travis Bickle (Robert De Niro) *Taxi Driver* (1976)
Where on Earth?: South Australia

Patchwork:

C	D	F	B	A	E
A	E	D	F	C	B
E	C	A	D	B	F
B	F	E	C	D	A
F	B	C	A	E	D
D	A	B	E	F	C

WHATEVER NEXT?

Which of the numbered alternatives comes next in this sequence:

| B | H | F | M | L | ? |

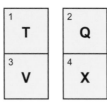

| 1 T | 2 Q |
| 3 V | 4 X |

COUPLINGS

Apart from two, every word listed below can be coupled with one of the others to make another word or phrase. Rearrange the letters of the two which can't be paired together to form one word, the name of an entertainment medium.

1 SHOOTING	2 CURTAIN
3 LOSE	4 CAPITAL
5 STORM	6 SKY
7 RAISER	8 GUN
9 CITY	10 HIGH
11 STAR	12 INVITE
13 FIGHT	14 THUNDER

Answer: _____

WEATHER for PESSIMISTS

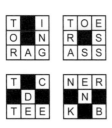

Today the weather will be: Wet with heavy rains causing flooding

IN CHAINS

This chain of letters contains the names of three fruits. The letters are in the correct order but need to be picked out.

C M H P A E L R N U R G Y M O

_____   _____

_____

JIGSAW CROSSWORD

Fit the blocks into the empty grid to form a complete crossword which, when finished, will be symmetrical, similar to the example seen here:

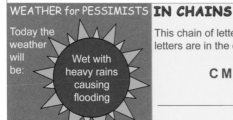

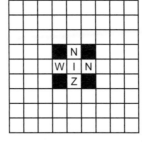

UNLIKELY CANDIDATE

BEST-DRESSED MALE

_____

181

WHAT'S IN A NAME?

How many words (other names included) can you make from the name:

HILDEBRAND

_____

_____

_____

_____

WHATEVER YOU DO, don't even THINK about...

Any of the following:

Broken teeth

Itchy Feet

Runny noses

BALANCING THE SCALES

Given that scales A and B balance perfectly, how many circles are needed to balance scale C?

BRIEF SURVIVAL GUIDE

PARENTING:

1 Practice saying "No" a lot
2 Add whiskey to a nightly feed
3 Send child to grandparents' house on a regular basis

TODAY'S GREATEST ACHIEVEMENT

Being happy ☐

Being spontaneous ☐

Cuddling the cat ☐

MASS HYSTERIAS

Today we are all going to:

Climb trees to hide from the folk next door.

PYRAMID PLUS

Every brick in this pyramid contains a number which is the sum of the two numbers below it, so that F=A+B, etc. No two bricks contain the same number, or just a zero, so work out the missing numbers!

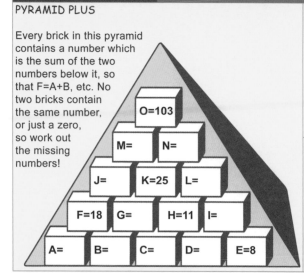

O=103

M= N=

J= K=25 L=

F=18 G= H=11 I=

A= B= C= D= E=8

STARTING LINE

Which three-letter word can be placed at the start, to form three seven-letter words?

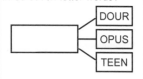

DOUR

OPUS

TEEN

SNOW WHITE

-v-

SLEEPING BEAUTY

WAYS TO PASS THE TIME ...

Making hay ☐

Cooing ☐

Calling for help ☐

SUDOKU

The numbers from 1 to 9 inclusive need to be placed into the grid below in such a way that every horizontal row and vertical column contains nine different digits. In addition, each of the nine blocks of nine smaller squares should also contain nine different numbers. The clues are the numbers already placed.

		9			1	3		8
1		4		7	5			
7			2		9	5		
	3			4	7		9	
	4	7				8	6	
	5		8	9			4	
		2	6		8			1
			9	3		4		7
3		8	7			2		

WORDFILLER

Can you place all the listed words into the grid below? One is already in place, to get you off to a good start.

4 letters
Ally
Ewer
Less
Lest
Okra
Sloe
Slur
Trot

5 letters
Corks
Elide
Elope
Evoke ✓
Jetty
Loose
Ovary
Ravel
Roots

Seedy
Steal
Track
Tryst
Vinyl

6 letters
Radius
Rotate

7 letters
Serpent
Sorcery

9 letters
Tortoises

Answers to puzzles on the previous page

Balancing the Scales: 11
Pyramid Plus: A=13, B=5, C=9, D=2, E=8, F=18, G=14, H=11, I=10, J=32, K=25, L=21, M=57, N=46, O=103.
Starting Line: CAN

JOIN THE DOTS

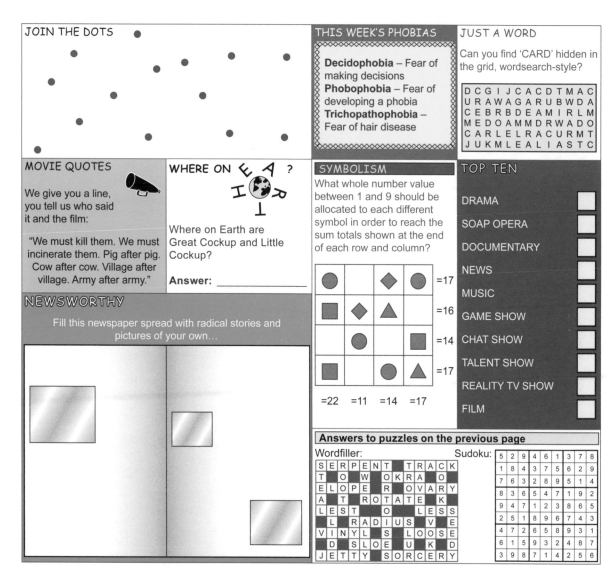

THIS WEEK'S PHOBIAS

Decidophobia – Fear of making decisions
Phobophobia – Fear of developing a phobia
Trichopathophobia – Fear of hair disease

JUST A WORD

Can you find 'CARD' hidden in the grid, wordsearch-style?

```
D C G I J C A C D T M A C
U R A W A G A R U B W D A
C E B R B D E A M I R L M
M E D O A M M D R W A D O
C A R L E L R A C U R M T
J U K M L E A L I A S T C
```

MOVIE QUOTES

We give you a line, you tell us who said it and the film:

"We must kill them. We must incinerate them. Pig after pig. Cow after cow. Village after village. Army after army."

WHERE ON FEAR?

Where on Earth are Great Cockup and Little Cockup?

Answer: _____

SYMBOLISM

What whole number value between 1 and 9 should be allocated to each different symbol in order to reach the sum totals shown at the end of each row and column?

●		◆	●	=17
■	◆	▲		=16
	●		■	=14
■		●	▲	=17

=22 =11 =14 =17

TOP TEN

DRAMA ☐

SOAP OPERA ☐

DOCUMENTARY ☐

NEWS ☐

MUSIC ☐

GAME SHOW ☐

CHAT SHOW ☐

TALENT SHOW ☐

REALITY TV SHOW ☐

FILM ☐

NEWSWORTHY

Fill this newspaper spread with radical stories and pictures of your own…

Answers to puzzles on the previous page

Wordfiller:

```
S E R P E N T   T R A C K
T   O   W   O K R A   O
E L O P E   R   O V A R Y
A   T   R O T A T E   K
L E S T   O   L E S S
  L   R A D I U S   V   E
V I N Y L   S   L O O S E
  D   S L O E   U   K   D
J E T T Y   S O R C E R Y
```

Sudoku:

5	2	9	4	6	1	3	7	8
1	8	4	3	7	5	6	2	9
7	6	3	2	8	9	5	1	4
8	3	6	5	4	7	1	9	2
9	4	7	1	2	3	8	6	5
2	5	1	8	9	6	7	4	3
4	7	2	6	5	8	9	3	1
6	1	5	9	3	2	4	8	7
3	9	8	7	1	4	2	5	6

PARTNERS IN RHYME

Each of the pairs below is a rhyme for a familiar phrase. Can you identify them?

1. Dan and Roy

_____

2. Buy and crow

_____

3. Pete and Heidi

_____

4. Kicks and groans

_____

We all know what we'd *like* to find on the internet and add to our Favorite folders, so make a list of all the websites you'd love to browse, if only they existed!

1 _____

2 _____

3 _____

4 _____

5 _____

6 _____

7 _____

8 _____

9 _____

10 _____

BRAINTEASER

In which year did the city of New Amsterdam change its name to New York?

TWO DOWN

Fit five of the seven listed words into the Across rows in the grid, so that the other two words read down the shaded columns numbered 2 and 3.

ADOPT   DAIRY
EMPTY   MEDIA
RIVER   SEPAL
     TAPER

NUMB-SKULL

Fit the listed numbers into the grid, crossword-fashion.

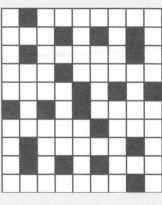

3 digits
105
374
526
805

4 digits
1426
1896
2504
4491
5917
6037
6504
6848
6939
7546
7732
8573

5 digits
24366
31256
55660
62317
64195
81937
93788
94958

7 digits
5470857
8560718

MUSIC TRIVIA

What was the name of Billy J Kramer's backing group in the 1960s?

Answers to puzzles on the previous page

Movie Quotes: Col Walter Kurtz (Marlon Brando) *Apocalypse Now* (1979)
Where on Earth?: Two hills in the Lake District of the UK
Symbolism:
Circle = 6, Diamond = 5, Square = 8, Triangle = 3.

Just a Word:

```
D C G I J C A C D T M A C
U R A W A G A R U B W D A
C E B R B D E A M I R L M
M E D O A M M D R W A D O
C A R L E L R A C U R M T
J U K M L E A L I A S T C
```

BOX CLEVER

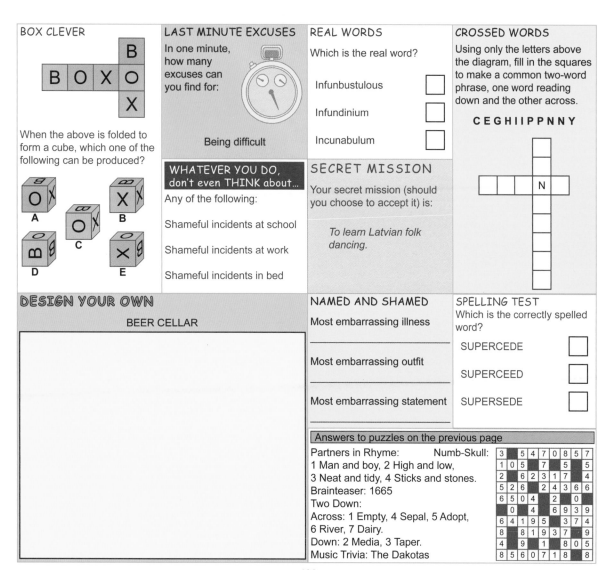

When the above is folded to form a cube, which one of the following can be produced?

A B C D E

LAST MINUTE EXCUSES

In one minute, how many excuses can you find for:

Being difficult

WHATEVER YOU DO, don't even THINK about...

Any of the following:

Shameful incidents at school

Shameful incidents at work

Shameful incidents in bed

REAL WORDS

Which is the real word?

Infunbustulous ☐

Infundinium ☐

Incunabulum ☐

SECRET MISSION

Your secret mission (should you choose to accept it) is:

To learn Latvian folk dancing.

CROSSED WORDS

Using only the letters above the diagram, fill in the squares to make a common two-word phrase, one word reading down and the other across.

C E G H I I P P N N Y

DESIGN YOUR OWN

BEER CELLAR

NAMED AND SHAMED

Most embarrassing illness

_____

Most embarrassing outfit

_____

Most embarrassing statement

_____

SPELLING TEST
Which is the correctly spelled word?

SUPERCEDE ☐

SUPERCEED ☐

SUPERSEDE ☐

Answers to puzzles on the previous page

Partners in Rhyme: Numb-Skull:
1 Man and boy, 2 High and low,
3 Neat and tidy, 4 Sticks and stones.
Brainteaser: 1665
Two Down:
Across: 1 Empty, 4 Sepal, 5 Adopt,
6 River, 7 Dairy.
Down: 2 Media, 3 Taper.
Music Trivia: The Dakotas

186

KEYWORD

Simply fill in the letters missing from the different words numbered 1-6 and enter them into the numbered boxes, to reveal the hidden keyword. Take care, however, as some may have more than one possible letter which could fit: for example S — M E might be either SAME or SOME.

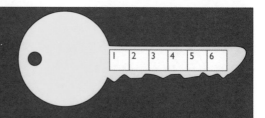

1	2	3	4	5	6

1 CAM—ER
2 COR—L
3 PLEA—ED
4 SOC—ET
5 SLE—T
6 —INDER

WORDSEARCH

Can you find all of the listed movie stars in the grid? Words may run in either a forwards or backwards direction, horizontally, vertically or diagonally, but always in a straight, uninterrupted line.

```
N V F S U K E M B O Y Y V
O Y O I D S C L O S E D G
O L R Z A L N M Z Y V N T
P S D H U E O K U E O A W
S X C M W G H N N R Y T O
R C Z M A W C I Y L P D L
E Q A Q O N N D O E N H A
H N J R E G E R K A R L Y
T V W L R R D Q R E L M T
I I B O E E G B W S L J I
W A B P N B Y I I I A L S
G E P N A D S G E U L F Y
U O S Y E L D P P R L P T
H G F T O O W F Z C E A Q
I N X H R G R H X V N G U
```

ALLEN
BORGNINE
BRANDO
CARREY
CHASE
CLOSE
CRUISE
DENCH
FORD
GABLE
GERE
GOLDBERG
HOPPER
KELLY
MURPHY
NEWMAN
OLDMAN
REYNOLDS
RYDER
TANDY
TAYLOR
WEST
WITHERSPOON

TOP FIVE

Best cars:

1 _____

2 _____

3 _____

4 _____

5 _____

SWEET BAD MUSIC

So who on earth was responsible for this lyric?

"Coast to coast
LA to Chicago"

SIMPLE AS A,B,C

In the grid, each row across, column down and diagonal line of six squares should contain two each of A, B and C. The clues relate to the squares only in that row or column. We give as many clues as we think you need (including any letters already in the grid), so can you place the letters correctly?

Across:
1 Each B is next to and right of a C.
4 The Cs are between the As.
6 The Cs are further right than the As.

Down:
2 Each A is next to and below a B.
3 Each A is next to and above a B.
4 The Bs are higher than the Cs.
5 The As are higher than the Cs.

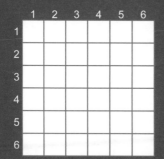

WORD LADDER

Change one letter at a time (but not the position of any letter) to make a new word – and move from the word at the top of the ladder to the word at the bottom using the exact number of rungs provided.

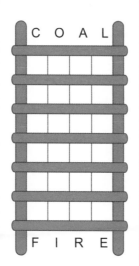

C O A L

F I R E

GOOD IMPRESSIONS

Can you pair up these door keys with the impressions of their ends?

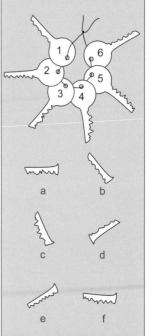

a   b

c   d

e   f

PRE-FAME NAME GAME

By what name do we know this famous person?

Prince Rogers Nelson

ALL AT SEA

What was the name of the raft used by Thor Heyerdahl in his 1947 expedition across the Pacific Ocean?

LEADING LADIES

Which of these women is walking the dog?

A

B

C

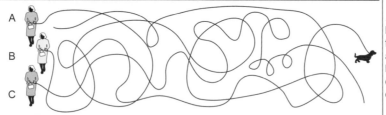

DO YOU KNOW...

...what historic feat of aviation happened on this date?

12
May
1926

WHAT DOES IT MEAN?

What is the meaning of the word

Mesonoxian

Answer: _____

WHAT'S IN A NAME?

How many words (other names included) can you make from the name:

CONSTANTINE

_____

_____

_____

_____

SUM THOUGHTS

What is the sum total of all of the following two-digit numbers?

91

43

46

11

65

51   39

USE YOUR IMAGINATION

Can you fill each of these boxes with a different fruit?

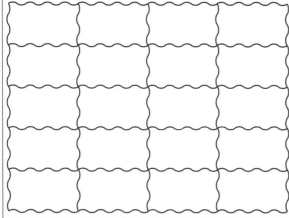

WHO AM I?

I'm a jerk, but listen!

I am:

_____

Answers to puzzles on the previous page

Word Ladder – One solution is: COAL, foal, foil, fail, fall, fill, file, FIRE.
Good Impressions: 1-d, 2-e, 3-a, 4-c, 5-f, 6-b.
Pre-fame Name Game: Prince
All at Sea: *Kon-Tiki*

Simple as A,B,C:

C	B	C	B	A	A
C	A	A	B	B	C
B	C	B	C	A	A
A	C	C	A	B	B
B	B	A	A	C	C
A	A	B	C	C	B

ON THE TILES

In this puzzle, the eight tiles on the right must be fitted into the pattern in the middle so as to form four words reading across and five words reading down. No tile may be rotated!

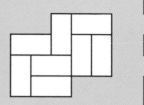

U	N

E
G

S
W

J	E

P	A

L
E

I
G

M	A

MY NEXT HOBBY

What:

How:

Why:

AMAZING

Can you work your way from the entrance at the top to the exit at the bottom of this maze?

ROUNDWORD

Write the answer to each clue in a clockwise direction. Every solution overlaps the next by either one, two or three letters and each solution starts in its numbered section.
The solution to the final clue ends with the letter in the first square.

1 Harmful, toxic
2 Ineffectual
3 Central meaning
4 US coin
5 Violent windstorm
6 Tyrannize
7 Devastate, destroy

Answers to puzzles on the previous page

Leading Ladies: Woman A
Do You Know…: Roald Amundsen and Umberto Nobile became the first men to cross the North Pole in an airship.
What Does It Mean?: Pertaining to midnight.
Sum Thoughts: 346
Who Am I?: Justin Timberlake

NAMED AND SHAMED

Untrustworthy

_____

Unworthy

_____

Unloved

_____

SPELLING TEST

Which is the correctly spelled word?

CONNOISSEUR ☐

CONOISSEUR ☐

CONNOISEUR ☐

STARTING LINE

Which three-letter word can be placed at the start, to form three seven-letter words?

☐ → FALL
☐ → HEAD
☐ → PROP

MUSIC TRIVIA

Which member of Crosby, Nash, Stills and Young started his career in a UK-based band?

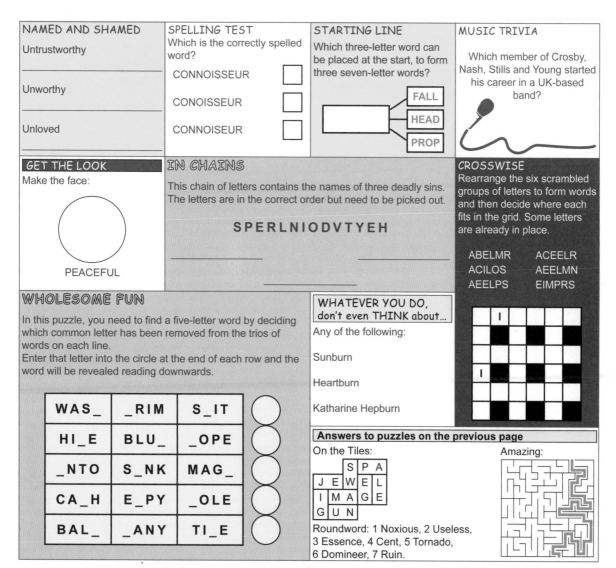

GET THE LOOK

Make the face:

◯

PEACEFUL

IN CHAINS

This chain of letters contains the names of three deadly sins. The letters are in the correct order but need to be picked out.

SPERLNIODVTYEH

_____   _____

_____

CROSSWISE

Rearrange the six scrambled groups of letters to form words and then decide where each fits in the grid. Some letters are already in place.

ABELMR   ACEELR
ACILOS   AEELMN
AEELPS   EIMPRS

WHOLESOME FUN

In this puzzle, you need to find a five-letter word by deciding which common letter has been removed from the trios of words on each line.

Enter that letter into the circle at the end of each row and the word will be revealed reading downwards.

WAS_	_RIM	S_IT	◯
HI_E	BLU_	_OPE	◯
_NTO	S_NK	MAG_	◯
CA_H	E_PY	_OLE	◯
BAL_	_ANY	TI_E	◯

WHATEVER YOU DO, don't even THINK about...

Any of the following:

Sunburn

Heartburn

Katharine Hepburn

Answers to puzzles on the previous page

On the Tiles:

		S	P	A
J	E	W	E	L
I	M	A	G	E
G	U	N		

Roundword: 1 Noxious, 2 Useless, 3 Essence, 4 Cent, 5 Tornado, 6 Domineer, 7 Ruin.

Amazing:

TOP TEN

- BOOK ☐
- MAGAZINE ☐
- LEAFLET ☐
- POSTER ☐
- NEWSPAPER ☐
- COMIC BOOK ☐
- PAMPHLET ☐
- PICTURE BOOK ☐
- LETTER ☐
- POSTCARD ☐

SPOT THE SAME

Only two of these modern abstract paintings are identical in every way: which?

THE NAME GAME

Can you complete the six words reading across in such a way as to reveal the name of a well-known person in the shaded columns?

	I	R			D
	O	R			E
	V	O			D
	A	R			H
	P	R			N
	A	I			T

NUMBER BOX

In this puzzle, simply use the hints given to enter nine different numbers 1-9 in their correct boxes.

2 is in a corner
7 is two squares above 3
6 is two squares right of 8
5 is two squares left of 1
4 is two squares above 6

NIGHT ANIMALS

Death's-head, large yellow underwing, peppered, and tiger are all types of which creature?

ON TARGET

The answers to the clues read from the outer circle to the center, all ending with the same letter. When you've finished, the letters in the shaded ring will give a word.

1 Incendiarism
2 The Devil
3 Wailing type of warning signal
4 Once more
5 Cloth made of flax
6 Country, capital Khartoum

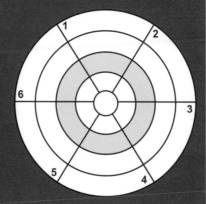

Answers to puzzles on the previous page

Spelling Test: CONNOISSEUR
Starting Line: PIT
Music Trivia: Graham Nash, in The Hollies
In Chains: Sloth, Pride and Envy
Wholesome Fun: PRISM

Crosswise:

S	I	M	P	E	R
O		A		N	
C	E	R	E	A	L
I		B		M	
A	S	L	E	E	P
L		E		L	

192

TOP FIVE

Best songs for flying:

1 _____
2 _____
3 _____
4 _____
5 _____

CELEBRITY WRESTLING

AL GORE

-v-

BILL GATES

UNFINISHED PICTURE

Can you complete this doodle?

QUOTE OF THE DAY

"Books are fatal; they are the curse of the human race. Nine-tenths of existing books are nonsense, and the clever books are the refutation of that nonsense."

Benjamin Disraeli

UNLIKELY CANDIDATE

SAINT

_____

DO YOU KNOW...

...what happened on this date?

6 December 1877

JIGSAW CROSSWORD

Fit the blocks into the empty grid to form a complete crossword which, when finished, will be symmetrical, similar to the example seen here:

R L E D
O V A C U E
M T C L

A V E R E
I I A
U M N C A L

S A U C H Y R E E S S E M I
P A R A N A E N
Y Y A N E E X T S D T E R

NAMED AND SHAMED

Biggest flirt

_____

Biggest tale-teller

_____

Biggest moaner

_____

MOVIE QUOTES

We give you a line, you tell us who said it and the film:

"There's no crying in baseball!"

WHERE ON EARTH?

Where on Earth is Muff?

Answer: _____

TODAY'S GREATEST ACHIEVEMENT

Not arguing ☐

Not crying ☐

Not laughing ☐

IN SHAPE

How many hexagons can you see here?

GET THE LOOK

Make the face:

INSANE

DOMINOLOGICAL

What is the value of the question mark?

?

PYRAMID PLUS

Every brick in this pyramid contains a number which is the sum of the two numbers below it, so that F=A+B, etc. No two bricks contain the same number, or just a zero, so work out the missing numbers!

O=130

M=   N=58

J=   K=   L=24

F=   G=   H=   I=

A=   B=   C=5   D=   E=3

WHO AM I?

Seen alive?
Sorry, pal!

I am:

_____

Answers to puzzles on the previous page

Do You Know...:
Thomas Edison made the first sound recording on his phonograph machine.

Jigsaw Crossword:

E		D	U	C	H	E	S	S
C	U	E		A		A		E
C		L	A	N	E	S		D
E	M	I	R		L	Y	R	E
N		O	V	A				N
T	E	R	M		T	E	X	T
R		E	A	V	E	S		A
I		A		I		P	A	R
C	A	L	U	M	N	Y		Y

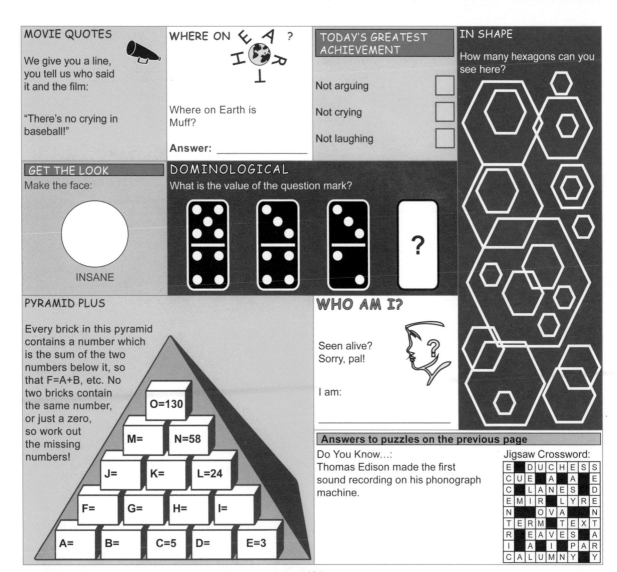

USE YOUR IMAGINATION

Can you write the name of a different color in each box?

SUM TOTAL

Place the digits 1-9, one per square, so that the sums are correct, according to the totals at the ends of the rows and columns. The calculations should be done in the order in which they appear, for example 6–2x5=20 should be read as 6–2(=4), then 4x5=20.

	+		x		=	96
–		x		+		
	x		–		=	19
+		+		x		
	–		x		=	10
=		=		=		
13		38		14		

THE LAST WORD

Which of the four lettered alternatives (a, b, c or d) should most logically fill the empty space? In other words, what have the listed words in common which is also shared by one of the alternatives?

ABBOT   BELLY

CHILLY   FLUX

GHOST   _____

a. Adept   b. Prime

c. Martyr   d. Shock

WORDWHEEL

Using only the letters in the Wordwheel, you have ten minutes to find as many words as possible, none of which may be plurals, foreign words or proper nouns. Each word must be of three letters or more, all must contain the central letter and letters can only be used once in every word. There is at least one nine-letter word in the wheel.

Nine-letter word: _____

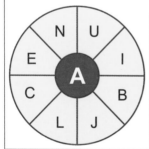

GET THE LEADER

Can you unscramble the anagram to reveal the leader?

Muddler of lands

Answer: _____

THIS WEEK'S PHOBIAS

Kathisophobia – Fear of sitting down
Homichlophobia – Fear of fog
Ostraconophobia – Fear of shellfish

REAL WORDS

Which is the real word?

MUGDEMP ☐

MUGDINT ☐

MUGWUMP ☐

Answers to puzzles on the previous page

Movie Quotes: Jimmy Dugan (Tom Hanks) *A League of Their Own* (1992)

Where on Earth?: Northern Ireland, Ireland and Pennsylvania

In Shape: 21.

Dominological: 1 at the top and 2 at the bottom; each domino flips 180 degrees and both numbers decrease by 1.

Pyramid Plus: A=1, B=16, C=5, D=8, E=3, F=17, G=21, H=13, I=11, J=38, K=34, L=24, M=72, N=58, O=130.

Who Am I?: Elvis Aaron Presley

ARRANGING THINGS

If you fit six of these seven words into the grid below, the word left over will appear reading down the shaded squares.

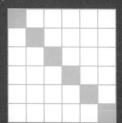

PACKET   PADDLE
PELVIC   PEOPLE
PILFER   PREACH
PROFIT

PAIR SHAPES

In the box below there are shapes in three different colors, red, white and blue. Any shape may have been rotated, but can you see which is the only shape to appear exactly twice in exactly the same color?

CAPITALS

The capital of

AUSTRALIA

is:

_____

UNFINISHED PICTURE

Can you complete the left half of this picture?

TOP TEN

CAR ☐

AEROPLANE ☐

BOAT ☐

BICYCLE ☐

WALKING ☐

SCOOTERS ☐

HORSEBACK ☐

TRUCK ☐

HOT-AIR BALLOON ☐

CARAVAN ☐

TODAY'S GREATEST ACHIEVEMENT

Breakfast ☐

Lunch ☐

Dinner ☐

NAME THAT SONG

We give you the first line, you name the song: ♪

I met her in a club down in Old Soho

Song: _____

MATCH THAT

Using just twelve matches, make a hexagon and six triangles – and possibly even a circle!

Answers to puzzles on the previous page

Real Words: Mugwump. A person who remains aloof from controversial issues.
Get The Leader: Donald Rumsfeld.
Wordwheel: The nine-letter word is JUBILANCE.
The Last Word: a. Adept – the letters in each word are in alphabetical order.

Sum Total:

9	+	7	x	6
−		x		+
4	x	5	−	1
+		+		x
8	−	3	x	2

COUPLINGS

Apart from two, every word listed below can be coupled with one of the others to make another word or phrase. Rearrange the letters of the two which can't be paired together, to form one word, the name of a European city.

1 MATTER	2 MOTH
3 HANDSHAKE	4 BREAK
5 BLOOD	6 BOTTLE
7 GOLDEN	8 RICE
9 RELATIVE	10 EATEN
11 WEEKEND	12 PUDDING
13 ROD	14 BLUE

Answer: _____

CODEWORD

This is a crossword puzzle in code. Every number represents a different letter of the alphabet and this number remains the same throughout the puzzle. Use the letters either side as well as the check-box below to keep a track on your progress.

	A									B	A	T		N
	B	8			1	10	18			17		1		O
	C	21	24	11	4		13	17	12	24	18	9		P
	D	6			10		26		5		22		Q
	E		16	1	4	9		26	25	24	20	19		R
	F	4		6		17	7	1		1		13		S
	G	18	1	22	10	14		18	10	9	1		T
	H	1		18		10			20			7		U
	I	7	19	1	1	23	1		20	10	15	1		V
	J													W
	K	1		9			1	2	1			10		X
	L													Y
	M	18	24	1	26	24	25		9	10	22	2		Z

Top row: 3 24 21 2 | 7 17 11 4 | 10 9

1	2	3	4	5	6	7	8	9	10	11	12	13

14	15	16	17	18	19	20	21	22	23	24	25	26

JOIN THE DOTS

BRIEF SURVIVAL GUIDE

SPORTS DAY:

1 Fake a broken leg

2 Fake a debilitating illness

3 Fake mental incapacity

WHERE ON ?

Where on Earth is Humptulips?

Answer: _____

Answers to puzzles on the previous page

Name That Song: *Lola*, The Kinks.
Arranging Things: Across (from the top): Paddle, Preach, People, Pilfer, Pelvic, Packet. Down: Profit.
Match That:
The circle is an optical illusion, right in the middle!

Capitals: Canberra.

Pair Shapes:

WEATHER for PESSIMISTS

Today the weather will be:

Hot enough to cause an itchy heat rash

WEATHER for OPTIMISTS

Today the weather will be:

Full of musical thunderstorms to enhance your mood

WAYS TO PASS THE TIME ...

Throwing peas ☐

Ironing socks ☐

Phoning friends ☐

THIS WEEK'S PHOBIAS

Aulophobia – Fear of flutes
Nyctophobia – Fear of night or darkness
Basophobia – Fear of walking

DESIGN YOUR OWN

FLOWER ARRANGEMENT

UNLIKELY CANDIDATE

PRIME MINISTER

_____

SECRET MISSION

Your secret mission (should you choose to accept it) is:

To spell out a rude word in giant letters in the windows of your building.

QUOTE OF THE DAY

"A letter is an unannounced visit, the postman the agent of rude surprises. One ought to reserve an hour a week for receiving letters and afterwards take a bath."

Friedrich Nietzsche

BRIEF SURVIVAL GUIDE

THROWING A PARTY:

1 Invite only friends you like and who like each other

2 Invite all your ex-partners and then leave them to it

3 Don't invite anyone at all

PICK 'N' MIX

Choose three words to describe your first love:

Exciting	Skinny
Interesting	Clever
Sexy	Cheerful
Overweight	Loving
Young	Funny

MASS HYSTERIAS

Today we are all going to:

Bark like angry dogs and chase the postman away in case he brings bad news.

Answers to puzzles on the previous page

Couplings: 2/10, 5/9, 7/3, 8/12, 11/4, 14/6. The letters of 1 and 13 can be rearranged to form ROTTERDAM. Where On Earth? Washington, USA.

Codeword:

J	U	N	K		W	O	M	B	A	T
I		E	A	R		O			E	
N	U	M	B		Y	O	G	U	R	T
X			A		F		Q		C	
	D	E	B	T		F	L	U	S	H
B		X		O	W	E		E		Y
R	E	C	A	P		R	A	T	E	
E		R		A		S			W	
W	H	E	E	Z	E		S	A	V	E
E		T		E	K	E			A	
R	U	E	F	U	L		T	A	C	K